## Praise for *From Prison to Paradise*

"Love of family and our Catholic faith shines through in this extraordinary work compiled by Kitty Cleveland, a gifted Catholic singer and witness to Divine Mercy. Having done parishes missions with Kitty, I know firsthand the powerful message of God's mercy and redemption that resonates in this story of her family. Both entertaining and moving, this book will inspire you to deeper fidelity to Christ and his Church!"
—**Very Rev. Chris Alar, MIC**, Provincial Superior, United States & Argentina, Marian Fathers of the Immaculate Conception

"No one who reads the amazing tale of Carl Cleveland within these pages will easily doubt the words of Leon Bloy that 'there are places in the heart which do not yet exist; suffering has to enter in for them to come to be.' Carl's candor and humor in the face of unjust imprisonment, his deep dive into the heart of divine mercy, and his encounters with Christ and his fellow inmates are unforgettable. A perfect read for any time, but especially for Lent."
—**Chris Baglow, PhD**, author of *Creation: A Catholic's Guide to God and the Universe*

"Kitty Cleveland's *From Prison to Paradise* is a profoundly moving testament to the transformative power of faith amidst unimaginable trials. Through her father's raw and heartfelt letters from prison, Kitty illuminates the journey from despair to hope, showing how surrendering to God's mercy can lead to deep healing and restoration. This book is not only a gripping narrative, but also a spiritual guide that invites readers to embrace trust in God's plan, no matter how dire the circumstances may seem. A compelling and faith-filled read, it will inspire anyone struggling to make sense of suffering or seeking renewal in their own spiritual life."
—**Danielle Bean**, author, speaker, podcaster

"*From Prison to Paradise* is a profound read that deeply moves the heart and mind. Kitty Cleveland and her father take you on a journey that leads to the depths and heights of human suffering and triumph, inspiring new generations of families to persevere in faith, hope, and love. This book is a vital witness of life-changing divine intervention, shining hope in a world that aches for it. Highly recommended!"
—**Kathleen Beckman**, evangelist and author

"Like a modernized account of things found in the lives of the saints, with drama, humor, trials and joy, *From Prison to Paradise* is an inspirational story of hope. Through thoughtful perspectives, Carl Cleveland's story of devastation and Kitty's sharing of her father's triumph, reveals our own crosses to be refining opportunities for true freedom in Christ."
—**Brian Butler**, executive director of Echo Community

"In writing *From Prison to Paradise*, Kitty Cleveland has revealed the interior lessons she learned by watching her father trust in God as he suffered a great injustice. I walked with Kitty during those trying years and can tell you that she entered her father's story herself. It became, in fact, 'their' story! This book will be a source of great encouragement and hope for those who are experiencing the trials of a loved one. What makes this book so unique is that it's from the perspective of a daughter. Kitty's generous transparency has become a loving invitation into a family richly nourished by her father's faithfulness. Prepare yourself to be inspired!"
—**Jeff Cavins**, creator of *The Great Adventure* Bible Studies

"Who knew that prison could become the path to paradise? By sharing her father's story, Kitty Cleveland offers readers a first-hand look at the redemptive power of suffering. Carl Cleveland's prison diary and letters are at times funny, insightful, thought-provoking, and achingly painful. Together they reveal the divine transformation of a soul through faith and the power of God's word. "My grace is sufficient," he heard again and again throughout his ordeal. From the first day of his unjust conviction we watch as that grace is poured out: turning an ordinary man and his family into an extraordinary and joyful witness to hope. *From Prison to Paradise* is a rich source of light and hope for those who suffer and for those who love them."
—**Sarah Christmyer**, general editor of the *Living the Word* Catholic Women's Bible and author of *Becoming Women of the Word*

"Absolutely incredible. I couldn't stop reading. This story will keep you riveted—and constantly marveling at the immense goodness of our God, whose mercy is limitless and whose providence is stunning. Five thousand stars!"
—**Claire Dwyer**, author of *This Present Paradise* and co-founder, Write These Words

"A deeply moving account of the triumph of Christ's grace in an ordinary family suddenly faced with horrendous circumstances. The diary entries of Kitty's father from inside federal prison are absolutely gripping. The whole family's roller-coaster drama of humiliation, heartache, trust, patience, disappointment, and ultimately joy, is a powerful confirmation of the truth that 'God works all things together for good for those who love him'(Romans 8:28)."
—**Dr. Mary Healy**, professor of Scripture, Sacred Heart Major Seminary

"I was privileged to hear my friend Kitty and her father, Carl, share their incredible testimony of God's power 'perfected in weakness' at the Holy Spirit Novena in May 2000, just weeks after Carl's release from prison. They shared, sometimes weeping openly, the 'fresh pain' of the suffering their family had endured, and the triumph of God's mercy manifested with astounding force in the midst of their personal calvary. Carl's story, finally told in writing, shouts to a world shrouded in doubt and darkness that God is real, that his mercy prevails, and that his love is victorious! If you need hope, read this book!"
—**Judy Landrieu Klein**, PhD, author of *Mary's Way: The Power of Entrusting Your Child to God* and *Miracle Man*

"I have been blessed to know Kitty Cleveland, her father Carl and mother Joey, as well as her sisters, for many years. I have prayed and suffered with them in their difficulties and rejoiced with them in their triumphs. It is inspiring to see in print this account of Carl's experience of utter humiliation of being wrongfully convicted and his ultimate release and vindication. Reading Kitty's loving tribute brings to mind the Scriptural rewards promised in Sirach 3:6: "He who honors his father shall have a long life." In this book, Kitty not only pays tribute to her earthly father, but also honors her heavenly Father for his grace and mercy in her family. May Kitty continue her beautiful and fruitful ministry of proclaiming God's goodness in word and in song!"
—**Patti Gallagher Mansfield**, author, *As By a New Pentecost*

"I certainly recommend this book. It is a gripping testimony of faith, hope, and love in the midst of a fallen and unjust world. And even more profoundly, it is a testimony to the faithfulness of our merciful God who works all things to the good for those who love him (Romans 8:28)."
—**Bishop Scott McCaig, C.C.**, Military Ordinary of Canada

"This book tells the powerful story of how a humbling divine appointment reveals the supernatural character of God's love and mercy. Through the journey, we gain a deeper appreciation for the overarching virtue of humility, through the witness of a man whose heart is deeply pierced and perfectly positioned to receive grace poured abundantly into his soul—a grace that would overflow into the hearts of his family, transforming them forever. The book's timely release aligns with the Church's Jubilee Year of Hope. What a gift it is to hold in your hands a diary of a faith journey whose effects offer hope to a world desperately in need of witnesses."
—**Andi Oney**, Hope and Purpose Ministries

"Anyone who knows Kitty Cleveland knows she has a beautiful voice and a big heart. Both shine through as Kitty shares the powerful story of the unjust imprisonment and miraculous release of her father, Deacon Carl Cleveland. Kitty's father's letters to his family are an often gut-wrenching, sometimes humorous, but always soul-searching window into one man's journey from the pain of imprisonment to the peace that passes understanding. Through it all runs the golden thread of the sustaining power of the word of God and the consoling peace of Divine Mercy. If you or someone you love have ever felt abandoned or forsaken by God; if you have ever felt that your situation is without hope, then read this book! In it, you will discover the abiding truth of Jesus' words to Saint Paul: 'My grace is sufficient for you, for power is made perfect in weakness' (2 Corinthians 12:9)."
—**Dr. Brant Pitre**, author of *Introduction to the Spiritual Life*

"In *From Prison to Paradise*, Kitty Cleveland captures the power of words written for another. Through her father's heartfelt and soul-searching letters from prison, Kitty shares her family's transformative journey in such a radically relational way that I felt I was walking with the Clevelands from injustice and betrayal through impossibility and despair to hope and joy, anxiously anticipating the next letter from Deacon Carl. With their gifted storytelling, this father-daughter duo shows how embracing the word of God leads to surrender, trust, consolation, and strength. Like Scripture, this book is infused with words of wisdom that warm you as you experience homecoming, deep peace, and perfect love. If you need a ray of hope to weather life's storms, *From Prison to Paradise* is for you!"
—**Kelly Wahlquist**, founder of WINE: Women In the New Evangelization, and author of *Wisdom from Women in Scripture*

# FROM PRISON TO PARADISE

A Story of Radical Trust in
God's Divine Mercy

## KITTY CLEVELAND

Foreword by *New York Times* Bestselling Author
**IMMACULÉE ILIBAGIZA**

Copyright © 2025 Kitty Cleveland

All rights reserved.

Published by The Word Among Us Press
7115 Guilford Drive, Suite 100
Frederick, Maryland 21704

wau.org

29 28 27 26 25     1 2 3 4 5

ISBN: 978-1-59325-730-9

eISBN: 978-1-59325-731-6

Unless otherwise noted, Scripture texts in this work are taken from the *New American Bible, revised edition* © 2010, 1991, 1986, 1970 Confraternity of Christian Doctrine, Washington, D.C. and are used by permission of the copyright owner. All rights reserved. No part of the *New American Bible* may be reproduced in any form without permission in writing from the copyright owner.

Scripture quotations marked as RSV are from The Catholic Edition of the Revised Standard Version of the Bible, copyright © 1965, 1966 National Council of the Churches of Christ in the United States of America. Used by permission. All rights reserved worldwide.

Excerpts from *Diary* are taken from *Diary of Saint Maria Faustina Kowalska: Divine Mercy in My Soul* (Stockbridge, MA: Marians of the Immaculate Conception, 2003). Numbers in parentheses indicate paragraph numbers in text.

"Press On" by Bob Filoramo: © Robert Filoramo (ASCAP)

Design by Rose Audette

No part of this publication may be reproduced, stored in a retrieval system, or transmitted in any form or by any means—electronic, mechanical, photocopy, recording, or any other—except for brief quotations in printed reviews, without the prior permission of the author and publisher.

Library of Congress Control Number: 2025930842

*For Dad*

# Contents

Foreword ..................................................................... 11
Introduction .............................................................. 13
1. A Fresh Start? ...................................................... 15
2. My Legal Career ................................................... 21
3. The Indictment .................................................... 25
4. The Trial ............................................................... 27
5. Forsaken ............................................................... 33
6. January 1998 ....................................................... 37
7. Kitty: A Turning Point ......................................... 44
8. February 1998 ..................................................... 46
9. March 1998 .......................................................... 54
10. April 1998 ............................................................ 60
11. May 1998 .............................................................. 65
12. June 1998 ............................................................. 69
13. July 1998 .............................................................. 75
14. August 1998 ......................................................... 84
15. September 1998 ................................................... 89
16. October 1998 ....................................................... 91
17. November 1998 .................................................... 96
18. December 1998 .................................................... 99
19. January 1999 ..................................................... 103
20. February 1999 ................................................... 105

| | | |
|---|---|---|
| **21.** | MARCH 1999 | 110 |
| **22.** | APRIL 1999 | 115 |
| **23.** | MAY 1999 | 118 |
| **24.** | JUNE 1999 | 121 |
| **25.** | JULY 1999 | 124 |
| **26.** | KITTY: GRACE FOR WHATEVER COMES | 127 |
| **27.** | JULY 22, 1999 | 129 |
| **28.** | AUGUST 1999 | 133 |
| **29.** | SEPTEMBER 1999 | 139 |
| **30.** | OCTOBER 1999 | 145 |
| **31.** | NOVEMBER 1999 | 148 |
| **32.** | DECEMBER 1999 | 150 |
| **33.** | JANUARY 2000 | 154 |
| **34.** | FEBRUARY 2000 | 156 |
| **35.** | MARCH 2000 | 158 |
| **36.** | APRIL 2000 | 161 |
| **37.** | KITTY: THE GREAT JUBILEE | 166 |
| **38.** | MAY 2000: CARL'S LAST LETTER | 170 |
| **39.** | PARADISE | 172 |
| **40.** | RESTORATION | 174 |
| **41.** | AN INVITATION | 180 |
| | POSTSCRIPT | 181 |
| | ACKNOWLEDGMENTS | 184 |
| | ABOUT THE AUTHOR | 185 |
| | SOUNDS OF PEACE | 187 |

# Foreword

I first met Kitty Cleveland in 2009 on a pilgrimage to Kibeho, Rwanda. I was instantly captivated by her blessed singing voice and the unforgettable testimony about her father's Divine Mercy miracle. I'm so happy that she has decided to share this testimony with the world.

Deacon Carl Cleveland was sentenced to ten years in prison for a crime he didn't commit. In this book, we watch him grapple with the trauma of losing everything he held dear—his family, law practice, ministry, financial security, reputation, and physical freedom. Kitty allows her father to tell his riveting story through his monthly letters from prison. These letters are a treasure, filled with humor, heartache, surprises, deep faith, and, ultimately, hope in God's merciful plan for each one of us, even when it seems that all is lost.

During the Rwandan genocide, when as a Tutsi I was hunted by my former friends and neighbors and forced into hiding for three months, I was filled with terror at the evil surrounding me. The only way I found peace was by immersing myself in the Holy Word and by praying the Rosary and the Divine Mercy Chaplet nonstop, from the moment I woke up till the moment I fell asleep. The grace of God during this time in deep prayer helped me to accept my situation, love others, and truly forgive my offenders—even as I learned that most of my family and friends, along with almost a million of my fellow countrymen, had been brutally murdered in the span of one hundred days.

Just as I was left to tell my story about the power of prayer and forgiveness when confronted with evil, so Kitty has been called to tell this story about her father's spiritual transformation in the midst of great suffering. In addition to her father's surrender to God's unpredictable plan for his life, we watch as Kitty embarks on her own journey of surrender and trust, leading to a far-reaching ministry of healing and encouragement. These stories give us hope that God is working all things for the good for those who love him and are called according to his purpose (see Romans 8:28). His grace truly is enough for us.

If you have ever struggled to make sense of suffering, to forgive, or to renew your faith, this book has something for you. Like my ministry and all works inspired by God, it was born from the cross. I pray it brings you healing and hope, especially as you bear your own crosses on the way to heaven.

—Immaculée Ilibagiza
Author of *New York Times* bestseller, *Left to Tell*

# Introduction

"Thank you, Jesus! THANK YOU, JESUS!" My father stood up behind the wheel of his little fishing skiff and threw his arms open. Tears streamed into his grey temples in the wind. After serving two years and four months of an unjust ten-year prison sentence, he was finally a free man.

Dad was released just three days before Divine Mercy Sunday, when Sr. Faustina Kowalska was officially canonized a saint. Our family credits this gracious favor to her intercession and to the Divine Mercy of Jesus. Just nine days before her canonization, we had begun praying the Divine Mercy Novena for Dad's release.

Dad had lost an appeal the previous year. But against all odds, he had been granted a hearing with the United States Supreme Court. In a rare *unanimous* judgment, the justices reversed his convictions and restored his precious freedom. We will never tire of thanking God for his Divine Mercy!

May this story—much of which is told through my father's letters from prison—enkindle in you a great hope that God knows you, loves you, and is infinitely merciful toward you.

# 1

# A Fresh Start?

On August 15, 1995, a sweltering summer day in southeastern Louisiana, I drove north from New Orleans across Lake Pontchartrain. Driving across the Causeway Bridge, the longest continuous bridge in the world, seemed appropriate. After three years of half-heartedly working as a lawyer with my father, I had gained the courage and clarity to chart a new path in counseling and music. I could barely contain the joy and lightness in my heart as I approached Southeastern Louisiana University, where I would begin my new studies.

The ancient live oaks on campus spread their branches in welcome as I walked to the registrar's office. After paying tuition and purchasing my books, I decided to call the law office to check for messages. Not everyone knew that I was no longer employed at Cleveland, Barrios, Kingsdorf and Casteix.

When the receptionist answered the phone, she sounded odd, stammering that she needed to put me on hold.

After a long delay, a paralegal finally picked up. "Is this Kitty?"

"Yes," I replied. "What's going on?"

Choking back tears, she said, "The FBI is here. They've seized all our files, and they won't let us leave."

"What?" I shouted incredulously.

"And, Kitty," she continued, "they want to talk to you."

I was the eldest of my parents' six daughters born over twenty-three years. My childhood was a simple one, mostly lived out in the couple blocks between home and St. Rita, our neighborhood Catholic church and school in Uptown New Orleans. My mother, Joey, and "Leontine, the Queen," our beloved housekeeper, held down the fort at home. My dad, Carl, worked long hours as a lawyer and was often gone on the weekends during hunting season.

Dad preferred to be the "fun" parent rather than the disciplinarian—taking us to get Plum Street snowballs in the summertime and to Tulane football games in the fall, or roughhousing on the bed most evenings till someone got hurt. Sometimes he took us duck hunting in the marshes of Lafitte, about an hour south of the city. Or he'd pile the whole family (plus our friends and his black Labrador retriever) into our station wagon and head to our humble camp in Ponchatoula on the Tangipahoa River.

My mom found it easy to relax in the country. She taught us how to spot fossils and banded agate among the gravel, forage for chanterelle mushrooms and muscadines, and identify the various flora and fauna we encountered. On summer nights we would catch lightning bugs in jars and swing in the hammock while the cicadas hummed in cacophonous rhythm. It was a little slice of heaven.

On Sundays in Ponchatoula, we would attend Mass at St. Joseph's and then head to my grandparents' home on the river for a delicious French Creole feast. We swam all afternoon at their

## A Fresh Start?

beach, then had naps and watched *The Wonderful World of Disney* in the back den.

Dad had excelled academically and in sports. He was six foot two and an imposing presence. His toughness served the Ponchatoula High School football team and led him to excel academically. Yet he consistently championed the underdog and the outcast, a quality that characterized his life both in and out of the courtroom.

Dad went to Tulane on a football scholarship and threw himself wholeheartedly into life at the Deke fraternity house. He finished his business degree in three years and moved on to law school, graduating with top honors in 1966. In the meantime, he married my adorable mother, Joey Lynn Walther, who was soon pregnant with me.

Dad practiced law with his father. The pressure was intense for a twenty-three-year-old with little experience. To cope with the stress, he routinely had a couple martinis during lunch and a scotch or two after work. It made him much more relaxed and affable. As soon as I was able, I was mixing drinks for him when he got home.

My dad would never think that he had a drinking problem, and few in New Orleans would question his drinking. I'm told that my step-grandfather even topped off my baby bottle with a little bourbon to put me to sleep (I still love a bourbon milk punch).

When my grandfather died from cancer at the age of fifty-seven, my father was heartbroken. Work at the firm became unbearable without his father's steady presence, and he began to look for a way out. He and my mom built a home in a new subdivision thirty minutes west of New Orleans, and he opened a new law firm.

Dad's personal office, which spanned the entire width of the second floor, had a twenty-foot-high ceiling, huge mahogany doors, and walk-through windows opening to an elegant wrought iron balcony typical of the French Quarter. Hanging behind his desk was a portrait of his maternal grandfather, architect Carl E. Woodward, a gentleman bad boy with twinkling blue eyes who had been the Governor General of the Isle of Capri during World War II. My father was named for him and aspired to be a swashbuckling adventurer just like him. During Mardi Gras, my dad would blow his grandfather's bugle to get the attention of the float riders, and we kids were delighted to be deluged with beads and trinkets on our perch over the parade route.

Although Dad's firm was considered small, they had a big reputation in the arena of lender liability and corporate contract violations. They defeated some of the best law firms in Louisiana and in the large legal centers of Dallas, Atlanta, Washington, DC, and New York. My dad took his clients' cases very personally, inevitably spinning the narrative as a grave injustice done to the powerless that needed to be vindicated by force of intellect and will. It was the story of David and Goliath played out over and over again. He always worked from that paradigm so he could feel passionate about his cases, even when inconvenient facts didn't favor that interpretation. His clients loved him for it.

Carl Cleveland pulled off some spectacular courtroom wins, but he also had some heartbreaking losses. The latter would make him uncharacteristically melancholic for weeks. To cope with the stress of his workload and his impending fortieth birthday, he bought a fancy sports car. He also started drinking daily for hours after work with his buddies. This, of course, concerned my mother and us girls.

Mom attended a Cursillo weekend, where she encountered the living love of God. This so profoundly impacted her that she plotted to get my father into going on his own Cursillo. Upon his return from that, Dad called a family meeting.

"Girls, I want to tell you about my weekend, which was wonderful. First of all, they took my car keys so I couldn't escape. I didn't like that one bit, but I decided that I would go ahead and make the best of it."

We thought that was pretty funny, given Dad's attachment to his sports car.

"On the second day," he continued, "one of the men shared his personal conversion story with us. He had everything a person could want—a beautiful family and home, a successful business, and more financial success than he could possibly ask for. But he was still deeply unhappy. He decided to leave his family and start a new life with another woman.

"In the end, this man lost everything that was important to him, leaving him more unhappy than ever and causing much pain to his family. He had failed to see and appreciate all of the gifts he already possessed."

At this point Dad's voice broke, and he began to cry. "I saw myself in this man's story," he confessed. I had never seen my dad cry before, and I was getting anxious about where this was headed.

"I thought my restlessness and unhappiness were all because you girls and your mom just didn't appreciate me enough, and I was even thinking about leaving and divorcing your mom."

We daughters all gasped at this frightening revelation.

"But the truth is that you girls and your mom are the greatest gifts God has ever given me! For so long I was trying to do everything on my own power, without God's help, to be the strong one. And now I know that Jesus is helping me carry my burdens, and I don't have to do it all alone anymore.

"Also," he continued through tears, "I'm really sorry for being such a jerk all these years."

We laughed and hugged Dad tight in a big group hug. His words, spoken from a place of love and vulnerability, were a joyous new beginning for my parents' marriage and for our family.

Dad soon joined a men's prayer group, began to read Scripture daily, and started praying with fervor for the first time in his life. This retreat experience led to three years of intense study that culminated in his being ordained a permanent deacon in the Archdiocese of New Orleans.

In addition to preaching the gospel and giving homilies, Dad ministered to men dying in the AIDS ward at Charity Hospital. He counseled young mothers in crisis pregnancies and would later baptize their babies. Along with my mother, he helped give the HEC (Handicapped Encounter Christ) retreats, where he discovered that those with disabilities and physical weakness had a lot to teach him about true strength.

After Sunday Mass, Dad would feed twenty people or more with venison from his latest bow-hunting trip or with his latest catch of redfish on the half-shell. Our door was always open.

Dad's temper softened, and his three-martini lunches were replaced by daily Mass at St. Patrick's, across from his office. His frat-house humor gave way to stirring homilies, often leading him (and the congregation) to tears. He joked that he might someday write a book about his conversion and call it *From Deke* (the name of his fraternity house in college) *to Deacon*.

# 2

# My Legal Career

My dad often talked longingly about his darling daughters joining him in the law practice, and almost all my work experience up through college was at his firm. I didn't much care for courtroom conflict or the tedium of statutes and procedure. My dream was to sing, preferably as a musical theater actress on Broadway. The bug had bit when I had my first solo in the seventh grade, singing "You Light Up My Life" by Debbie Boone.

I continued singing and doing musicals throughout high school. And when I won the school talent show with "The Way We Were," I was ready to pack my bags for Julliard or New York University. But God had other plans.

In the summer of 1983, just before the start of my senior year, I attended a retreat. Some girls there shared that they had been "baptized in the Holy Spirit" over the summer, and their faith had come alive. On the last night, when everyone was going out for pizza, I asked them to stay behind and help me pray for the same thing.

The five of us held hands and began to pray the Our Father, with the hope that the Holy Spirit would descend upon us in a fresh and powerful way. Interiorly I begged, "God, if you exist, I *really* want to know." It was the first adult prayer of my life, I suppose, and I prayed it with all my heart.

In that instant, an ecstatic joy and warmth shot through my entire being, and I began weeping. It was an experience of homecoming, deep peace, and perfect love! The veil between heaven and earth seemed to mystically part, as I experienced the presence of this loving God living *in me*. I knew concretely that no matter what happened to me in this life, that Love would be there to meet me when I died.

We continued praying and rejoicing till the rest of the girls returned, and then it happened to many of them, too. It was an astonishing sight as thirty or so teenage girls wept and laughed and prayed for hours into the night.

When I got home, I embraced my parents with wild abandon and told my little sisters that I was sorry for all the times I had been mean to them. I added that I loved them and that God was real and loved them, too. I began to devour Scripture searching for understanding about who Jesus was and what was happening to me. And my dreams of singing on Broadway faded as I searched for ways to convey through music the reality of the love of God.

Tulane University was the easy choice for college. It was a short distance from home, and the musical theater program was top notch. The Catholic student center was also nearby, and there I could nurture my fledgling faith and hang out with my friends.

But I quickly settled into the Tulane party culture, spending much more time in the bars and Greek life than in prayer or songwriting. And while I continued to take voice lessons, sing in choirs, and perform in musical theater, I agreed with my earnest father that a Christian music career was "impractical."

## My Legal Career

His dream for me—and for all my sisters—was to practice law with him. With a twinkle in his eye, he envisioned calling the firm Carl's Angels.

I graduated from Tulane and worked for a year as a paralegal while I discerned my future. During that time, I attended my own Cursillo in the hope that God would speak to my anxious heart about his plans for my life. At the end of the weekend, it was clear: God was calling me to sing for him and about him.

I tried a Christian singing competition at the Baptist Seminary that offered a record deal, but I totally bombed. I had no idea how to hear God about this, figuring he must not want me to do it if it was this hard. My default was to ask my dad's opinion, and his opinion was that I should be a lawyer. Period. He was thrilled when I finally caved and entered LSU Law School in the fall of 1989.

My mother supported my singing dreams, but her hands were full. Not only was she busy raising several daughters and working in a crisis pregnancy center, but she had recently learned that she was expecting daughter number six. It had been nine years since her last pregnancy, and she was now forty-four years old. Caitlin would become the family favorite and my father's sidekick.

I passed the Louisiana Bar Exam and was ready to practice law. However, the country was in the midst of a deep recession, and I couldn't get a job. I was depressed, especially because I had spent seven years preparing for a career I didn't really want. My father agreed to hire me on a temporary basis, and I was glad to have a job.

As an antidote to my depression, I started auditioning for musical theater productions, and thus I met Mel, a handsome clarinet player from the orchestra. We worked together on several plays and started dating seriously. At our law firm Christmas party, Mel got up the nerve to ask my father the Big Question. It was only the second time they had met. My dad jokingly replied, "And you are?" Then he said, "We'll talk."

Dad never lost an opportunity to deliver a memorable homily. The next day at Mass, he stood at the ambo to preach on the Annunciation. "On this very special day, Mary gave her fiat to God," he began, "and the world was never the same." Then he paused and said, "As a matter of fact, I had the opportunity to give my own fiat last night when my daughter's boyfriend asked my permission to marry her."

"Oh, no!" I thought.

I felt my face flush as he leaned around to make eye contact with me in the choir.

"So, Kitty, the answer is . . . yes!"

The entire congregation erupted in applause as I hid my face behind the sheet music.

# 3

# The Indictment

After several months of tedious work at the firm, I was ready to move on to something more fulfilling. In a last-ditch effort to keep me in the practice of law, my dad told me about a client who operated one of the largest and most successful truck stops in the south. Our firm had helped him with real estate contracts in the past. Now that gambling was legal in Louisiana, the client wanted help obtaining a license to operate a few slot machines at his truck stop.

The license was obtained, and the slot machines became a huge success. The client was so thrilled with the additional income that he wanted to expand into a nearby hotel and other truck stops. And he wanted my help.

Helping the client "for a few months" ended up taking more than two years, as he attempted to acquire more and more truck stops across the state. Desperate to escape, I scheduled a silent retreat at the peaceful Cenacle retreat house on the southern shore of Lake Pontchartrain, where I had written my first song in high school.

As I found silence for prayer, as well as the listening ear of a compassionate nun, I knew that God was calling me to do work that was both healing and life-giving. I was willing to cut my losses and even disappoint my father for the possibility of finding meaningful, creative work.

I wrote a letter to my dad that weekend, conveying my deep unhappiness with practicing law and my discernment about God's plan for my life: to get a master's degree in counseling and to pursue my Christian singing and songwriting career.

On Monday morning, I handed my father the letter with a serene resolve that I had never known before. He and our client did their best to dissuade me, but I could not be moved. For the first time in my life, I was clinging to God instead of my dad, and I was filled with eager anticipation as the future opened up for me once again.

And then the FBI showed up.

The devastation at my dad's office happened on the very day I began my new career. Unbeknownst to us, our client had been selling shares in his operation to state politicians as insurance against unfavorable legislation. While it was legal for these politicians to own an interest in the enterprise, my father would never have condoned currying favor with them.

# 4

# THE TRIAL

Six defendants were tried together: my father, his client, the client's daughter, their CPA, and two prominent state senators. I consider it miraculous that I wasn't indicted, given the amount of time I had spent working exclusively on this client's leases and contracts. I told my dad that I felt as if God had lifted me out of mortal danger at the very last second, bringing me to safety as I followed his lead. My dad said that, while he was grateful I was spared, it seemed the exact opposite had happened to him.

Our family was confident that things would all work out once the facts were revealed at trial. In the meantime, my father voluntarily resigned as a deacon so as not to cause scandal. He tried to stay focused on the work that he still had to do at the office. Hundreds of friends and parishioners sent supportive letters and assurance of their prayers.

I threw myself into graduate school as if my life depended on it, and I found great fulfillment there. It was as though I had been "writing with the wrong hand" for my six years in law, and now I was finally getting to write with ease using my dominant hand. I loved the coursework, my teachers, and the experience I gained in my mental health counseling internship on campus. My professors offered me a job teaching in the department as soon as I received my MEd in Counseling in May 1997. They hired me to teach Career Planning, of all things!

The month after I graduated, in the summer of 1997, the trial was finally scheduled to begin. By this point, my father's law firm had been completely dismantled and his reputation was destroyed.

A couple weeks before the trial, a spirit-filled friend from New Orleans offered to pray with my dad. Patti Gallagher Mansfield had been a participant in the historic "Duquesne Weekend" in 1967, which sparked the Charismatic Renewal in the Catholic Church. My father jumped at the chance to pray with her. She began by reading a mysterious Scripture passage by St. Paul:

> And to keep me from being too elated by the abundance of revelations, a thorn was given me in the flesh, a messenger of Satan, to harass me, to keep me from being too elated. Three times I besought the Lord about this, that it should leave me, but he said to me, "My grace is sufficient for you, for my power is made perfect in weakness." I will all the more gladly boast of my weaknesses, that the power of Christ may rest upon me. For the sake of Christ, then, I am content with weaknesses, insults, hardships, persecutions, and calamities; for when I am weak, then I am strong. (2 Corinthians 12:7-10, RSV)

This Scripture passage was hardly a consolation in the moment, as it pointed to great suffering still to come. My parents returned home and prepared for the coming trial as much as they could, but they had a terrible sense of foreboding.

# The Trial

As we geared up for the first day of the trial, a contingent of family, friends, lawyers, and experts set up camp at my father's office across from the downtown New Orleans federal courthouse. There we tried to keep spirits lifted and bodies fed.

My sweet sister Caroline, just fifteen years old, accompanied my dad each day to the courtroom and often sat alone. The rest of us were either potential witnesses, working out of state, or, in Caitlin's case, too young to attend. Tension was high in the camera-packed courtroom as the numerous lawyers laid out their cases.

Weeks into the trial, it was time for my dad to take the stand. After hours of testimony, all reports were that my dad was brilliant, calmly explaining complex issues in layman's language. Even the press began to question why he was being prosecuted, and witnesses called by the prosecution ended up supporting my father's innocence.

That evening we chartered a bus for our large group of lawyers, family, and faithful friends in order to celebrate the impending victory at a local restaurant. We were happy to bide our time in the remaining days till my father was cleared and life could return to normal. I repeatedly listened to the "William Tell Overture" on my boom box, queuing up the grand finale so I could blast it across Lafayette Square as soon as he was exonerated.

Archbishop Hannan, the well-loved retired archbishop of New Orleans and World War II hero, took the stand as my father's character witness, which was a great comfort to us. The defense team had also hired twelve people to sit in the courtroom and listen to the evidence that the jury was hearing during the seven-week trial. These "shadow jurors" didn't know which side had hired them, but they all exonerated my dad and questioned why he was even a defendant.

After weeks of testimony and nine days of deliberations, the jury returned with their verdicts. It was July 1997. Adrenaline and anxiety were high.

My parents had gone to Mass early that morning, as they did every day, to pray for God's protection and guidance. And when the lector opened to the assigned Scripture passage, they were astonished as he began to read from 2 Corinthians 12:9, the identical passage prophetically given two weeks earlier by Patti Mansfield: "My grace is sufficient for you, for power is made perfect in weakness."

A shiver went up my father's spine.

Now as I walked into the overflowing courtroom next to my dad, he whispered, "Kitty, if there's even one guilty verdict against me, my life is over." He walked resolutely to the front of the courtroom and sat at the defense table. The room was so packed with the media that my mother, sisters, and I struggled to find seats. We held our breath and held hands when my father's name was called to hear his fate. The first count was read and the verdict announced:

"Guilty!"

The courtroom erupted in noise and chatter. My heart shattered, and I could barely breathe. My father sat in the chair with his back to us, head hanging down.

"Dad! *Dad!*" I cried.

The words caught in my throat as I tried to connect with him a few feet away. He couldn't hear me over the noise, so I shouted out, loudly enough for the judge and jury to hear. *"We believe in you, Dad!"*

The judge pounded her gavel and demanded order in the court so that the rest of the verdicts could be read.

"As to count two, guilty!"

## The Trial

I buried my face in my hands and began to sob. I didn't know how we were going to make it through the next minute, and I was starting to panic. I searched the faces of the jurors for some kind of explanation, but they wouldn't look at us. Thoughts raced through my mind. *What's going to happen to my dad? How will my mom and little sisters survive? Is this really happening to us?*

As more guilty verdicts were read and I cried out to God in anguish, a surprising grace was given to me. The Divine Mercy image of Jesus came clearly into focus, as though someone was holding it right in front of my face. During the trial I had been reading St. Faustina's diary, which I found deeply consoling and inspiring. And this was the image of Jesus that she had commissioned after he instructed her to do so. It was for a very special purpose: to prepare people to turn back to him during this time of mercy before he comes in his justice.

Sr. Faustina Kowalska was a Polish nun and mystic born in 1905. She died at the age of thirty-three in Krakow, after writing down profound visions and conversations she had with the Lord. She relates in her diary how he appeared to her with rays of white and red light emanating from his chest, signifying the blood and water that gushed forth from his pierced heart, "the depths of his tender mercy."

Jesus asked Faustina to have this image painted. The words "Jesus, I trust in You" were to be at the bottom of the image. It was a promise that this image of Jesus' mercy would be a source of many blessings for those who would meditate upon it.

The messages Faustina received, including a request for a new Feast of Divine Mercy on the Sunday after Easter and this Divine Mercy image itself, would become hallmarks of the papacy of Pope St. John Paul II. Years later he would die on the eve of

Divine Mercy Sunday, right after the vigil Mass was celebrated at his bedside.

As I sat there crying in the courtroom with this divine vision in front of me, I kept praying those words over and over again, *"Jesus, I trust in you! Jesus, I trust in you!"* I couldn't imagine how, but I knew that Jesus would see us through this nightmare. And then, slowly, I felt a ray of peace penetrate my soul.

---

> The graces of My mercy are drawn by means of one vessel only, and that is—trust. The more a soul trusts, the more it will receive. Souls that trust boundlessly are a great comfort to Me, because I pour all the treasures of My graces into them. I rejoice that they ask for much, because it is My desire to give much, very much. (*Diary*, 1578)

---

# 5

# Forsaken

We had not prepared for this outcome. My parents had not even discussed the possibility of conviction. Dad's attorneys and even the press were dumbfounded. Dad was ultimately found guilty of ten RICO (racketeering and corruption) violations, which were internally inconsistent and made no sense.

When we were allowed to leave the courtroom, reporters clamored around my dad to film his reaction for the six o'clock news, then offered their condolences off camera. My father was numb with shock. He told one reporter that he'd just been handed a virtual death sentence.

Since the formal sentencing was still several weeks away, Dad was released on bond. That night I went to check on him before I returned home with Mel. I found Dad lying in bed with his back to me. As I stood in the doorway, I heard him cry out in despair, "My God, my God, why have you forsaken me?" (Mark 15:34).

Those sorrowful words, words that Jesus spoke from the cross, pierced my heart. I was helpless to console him, and it felt like God had completely abandoned us.

My father was ultimately sentenced to ten years and one month in federal prison, with the remote possibility of being paroled one year early. Additionally, he was ordered to forfeit more than $1.5 million in assets to the government—assets he had never received. This would entail the loss of everything my parents owned—including our family home—and then some.

Hundreds of friends and former clients wrote to the trial judge to ask her for leniency. In some cases, nonviolent criminals are allowed to stay home pending the appeal. The judge denied our requests and ordered that my dad report to federal prison in Pensacola, Florida, right after Thanksgiving.

When that terrible day came, Dad decided that he would show up a few hours earlier than required so that he could maintain some semblance of autonomy. My mother, a few of my adult sisters, and I made the three-and-a-half-hour drive to the prison. We were all terribly sad and worried about his safety. One of my sisters was inconsolable.

We watched in shock as Dad walked to the prison entrance. He didn't turn around as the door closed behind him. We began the drive home in stunned silence. We weren't fifteen minutes away before we got a call that the judge had issued a stay, and we were to go back and pick him up! What a mixture of agony and relief we experienced in that short amount of time.

After a few weeks of deliberation, the judge ordered my father to return to prison on December 29, 1997. This time we all agreed that his friend Dan would take him. My sister Beth, who had not been on the first trip, also accompanied him. The rest of us just couldn't go through it again.

One week after his departure, we were permitted to visit for the first time. We stood in a long line with other visitors, each of whom had to be painstakingly cleared for entry. No one spoke much or made eye contact. Our personal belongings had to fit in a clear ziploc bag, which was searched thoroughly for contraband. Finally we were admitted to the waiting room.

After confirming our identities, including that of little Caitlin, my father was called over the intercom. He came wearing a green jumpsuit, his official identity now reduced to a number on his chest: 25306-034. As we took in this new reality, I developed an ocular migraine that caused me to go partially blind, as though my eyes were trying to block out what I was seeing. Much of our visit was spent in numb silence, though we did our best to console each other.

When it was time to go, we each hugged Dad tightly and tried to be brave. As he left the visiting room through a guarded door, we pushed through the double glass doors that led to the outside world and began walking in silence to the car.

Caitlin jumped up on a brick retaining wall that lined the walkway leading to the parking lot. She teetered along it with her arms out, a playful reprieve from the realization that we would visit this hellhole most weekends for the next ten years.

Rather than express her heartache outright, Caitlin intentionally slipped off the wall, finding in her scraped knee a reason to cry out. It wasn't fair, life wasn't fun anymore, and *Dad was gone*. Because this was our first visit, we didn't know that our father was enduring a dehumanizing body-cavity search just a few feet away, and he was listening helplessly to Caitlin's agonizing cries. This was one of the darkest moments of his life.

But soon some rays of hope would emerge.

... if God sends such great suffering to a soul, He upholds it with an even greater grace, although we are not aware of it. One act of trust at such moments gives greater glory to God than whole hours passed in prayer filled with consolations. (*Diary*, 78)

# 6

# January 1998

As of 11 a.m. today, January 5, I have been in prison for one full week. What a week! For the first forty-eight hours, I truly experienced the "dark night of the soul," a deep sense of sadness and despair.

Over and over I asked myself and my God how this could have happened to me. The legal system I have devoted thirty-two years to serving faithfully, fully believing in its fairness, has let me down. I am puzzled and perplexed at what could possibly have led to the merciless destruction of everything that is precious to me.

Countless times, two passages from Mark's Gospel have come to mind. First, the agony in the garden, when Jesus confessed to Peter, James, and John, "My soul is sorrowful even to death" (Mark 14:34). This describes exactly how I feel.

The second passage is Jesus' cry from the cross shortly before he died: "My God, my God, why have you forsaken me?" (Mark 15:34). Though Jesus prayed fervently to his all-powerful Father to let the cup of his suffering and death pass from him (14:36), the Father's response to his beloved Son was, "No." It was necessary for Jesus to be unjustly tried, convicted, and executed so that his power could be revealed in his resurrection and we could be saved from eternal death.

Though hundreds of faithful family and friends have joined in my passionate plea to our loving God to let the "cup" of public humiliation, professional ruin, separation from family and friends, and ten years of incarceration pass from my life, God has said "No" to me.

As my thoughts became dark and desperate this week, I read the first few psalms. The first promises that God "knows the way of the just" (Psalm 1:6). The third psalm speaks of trust in God during times of danger, despair, and injustice. The fourth desperately asks, as I do, "How long, O people, will you be hard of heart? Why do you love what is worthless, chase after lies?" (4:2). The psalmist urges trust in God when we are suffering and promises that those who trust him will each day be able to "lie down and fall asleep asleep" in peace (4:8). Miraculously, I can usually sleep peacefully in the midst of the chaos that is a fact of life here.

The fifth psalm is an ardent prayer for God's help from someone in a desperate situation. The psalmist's tormentors are described in a way that my prosecutors might also be described: "There is no sincerity in their mouth; their heart is corrupt. Their throat is an open grave" (5:9).

The sixth psalm is a prayer for help in a time of deep distress. The psalmist describes his body and soul as "shuddering" at what is happening to him (6:3, 4); he "drench[es] [his] bed with tears" and "soak[s] [his] couch with weeping" (6:7). His eyes are "dimmed with sorrow" and his body is "worn out" (6:8). After a lifetime of a manly absence of tears, I find myself crying often when I am alone.

## January 1998

It occurs to me that these ancient Hebrews are describing my pain and my recent life experiences passionately and eloquently. What a helpful insight: we all suffer! My next thought is whether there could be a significant purpose in this seemingly unjust suffering.

The seventh psalm is David's plea for divine help. He fears he will be torn to pieces like a lion's prey, with no one to rescue him. He begs God for justice because he is an innocent and just man. He vows to sing God's praise if he is rescued.

These ancient expressions of sadness and despair on the one hand and joy and justice on the other have become intensely relevant to my life. Perhaps you wonder, as I do, why people who strive to serve a loving God have to suffer unjustly. In Romans 8:22, St. Paul observes that all of humanity and all of nature must suffer. And since Jesus willingly suffered, how can any of us who follow him expect to avoid a similar fate? Furthermore, as one commentator observed, "It is out of suffering and pain that the kingdom of God arrives."

In other words, we eventually find God and might lead others to God by example—that is, by suffering without self-pity. And our suffering will ultimately end, our lives will be resurrected, and joy will return.

The realization that there is a purpose in my suffering, perhaps even a great and as yet unseen purpose, has empowered me to take heart. Hope has returned. Faith is rekindled. Some brief moments of joy peek out through the dark clouds.

I must say that my arrival to prison as a voluntary "self-surrender" was the worst day of my life. As I entered the prison compound at a Pensacola Navy base, everyone stared at the "new fish." Within minutes I was stripped naked, processed, and issued a fluorescent orange, one-piece jumpsuit and oversized slip-on canvas shoes. No underwear. No belt. No shoelaces or socks. My only belongings permitted were a Bible, my glasses, and my wedding band. I was later given permission to have a rosary and crucifix.

After several hours in an isolation cell, I was assigned a bunk and dumped into the general population. As a middle-aged, overweight white lawyer, I stuck out like a sore thumb among the young tattooed drug dealers who make up the majority of the prison population here. Many extended a helping hand as I staggered around in a tearful daze.

## Daily Life for Inmate 25306-034

In an attempt to make the most of my situation, I have invented the 1998 Prison Diet. I have eliminated salt, bread, fats, salad dressings, butter, sugar, and all drinks except water and skim milk at breakfast. In my first seven days, I am down about seven pounds.

We get served lots of bread, pasta, rice, potatoes, and canned vegetables. There is not much meat or seafood. The prison budget for meals is $2.61 per prisoner per day. Although this is less than $.90 a meal, it works because all labor is supplied by inmates.

I asked one "chef" if we had gumbo, and he responded in the affirmative. I then asked how they made their roux. His response was "What's a roux?" I have now volunteered to be a guest chef in charge of sauces, gravies, and gumbos. The ingredients for real food are all here.

Everyone here has a job. Most of us are janitors and gardeners. There are many other jobs—in horticulture, food service, carpentry, engine repair, safety, and so on. The off-base jobs involve lots of personal freedom but lead to the most problems when the rules are broken or stretched. Today's rumor is that I will be confined to the base because my sentence is so long, at least until the Bureau of Prisons (hereinafter "BOP") is satisfied I won't leave.

My age, education, skills, and experience should qualify me for a "good" job, but I probably will be a grass cutter. I would like any job that involves real work, to make the time pass more quickly and, I hope, achieve some sense of accomplishment. At present I am still in Admission and Orientation. This involves looking purposeful and staying out of trouble but basically doing nothing. I've had all of this I can stand. God, send me a real job, please!

## Dorm Life

I share a room with eight men, and all have extended themselves to me since I had nothing, knew nothing, and was clearly in a state of shock. They supplied a tour of the base, books, magazines, and toiletries.

The room is small and crowded but fairly clean and comfortable. There are no bars or locks on the doors. After several sleepless nights, I now sleep soundly from about 10:00 p.m. to 5:30 a.m. I have a top bunk by a window.

Each of us has a small metal locker with a combination lock. Security is not a problem. My twenty dollars in quarters and my stamps are safe. My uniforms and windbreakers all have name tags. Usually the lockers are left open unless we all leave the room.

There are two bath and toilet facilities on my floor, which are usually crowded and filthy. Amazingly, the showers are great! The hot water never runs out (the way it does at home!), and the temperature is constant.

Workout and recreation facilities are plentiful, as are libraries and classes. I'm on the waiting list for typing and computer classes and enrolled in a stretching and "abs" aerobics class. I'm also involved in several prayer groups and in Toastmasters.

Everyone says staying busy is the key to sanity, peace of mind, and time passing quickly and smoothly.

The chapel, only six months old and built with inmate labor, is better than those of many retreat facilities. The chaplain is a full-time Catholic priest named Fr. Joe. He has been great to me. He permitted Joey and Kitty to lead the music at Sunday Mass. He loved them and asked them to return. Their beautiful voices really lifted my spirits.

Fr. Joe ministers to all inmates—Catholic, Protestant, Jewish, Muslim, and Buddhist. I am in the daily Rosary group and have been invited to join the predominantly black nondenominational prayer group. I have great hope that there will be a place for me in the chapel programs eventually.

## Friends

I have learned quickly that prison is the place to be pleasant but private. It is not the place to make new lifelong friends. The statistics show that many of the inmates are con men looking to get something out of someone. Well over one-third of the inmates are "snitches," having bargained for light sentences in exchange for testifying against others. There are exceptions, of course. I have met some men who seem trustworthy and decent.

We have mail call at 5 p.m. every day. I can receive letters (which are all opened and read before delivery), photographs, paperback books, and magazines. Today I got eleven letters. What a great surprise! I will answer every one ASAP, even though I have only written a few non-business letters in my life.

## January 1998

Attorneys working on my case can visit any time by calling and asking for my case counselor. Family members are all okay to visit during regular visiting hours. If anyone else would like to visit me, I would welcome you. The visiting hours are Friday, 5–9 p.m.; Saturday and Sunday, 8 a.m.–3:30 p.m.

### God Is with Me

All in all, the facilities, meals, men, staff, and chapel are first rate. I am convinced that my life here is similar to a monk's life. I rise early, pray all fifteen decades of the Rosary, minister to men in great need, work hard at a menial job, read Scripture, eat bland food, study, and pray fervently. My life has no ups or downs—no phone calls, problems, or pressures.

The challenge now is to add a sense of purpose. I believe that I have found that in the psalms I happened to read. We all suffer. It is not for me to decide whether this cup shall pass in less than ten years. I will do my best to patiently endure whatever comes.

God has not abandoned me. He holds me in the palm of his hand and has rewarded me with a sense of peace that defies human understanding. After only seven days, I sleep soundly straight through the night. And each day holds some new adventure.

My love and prayers and undying appreciation are extended to each of you who have been so faithful, patient, and kind to Joey, the girls, and me. I fervently hope that, when suffering strikes any of you, you will call upon me to support and encourage you. Remember that you need not cry for me. My suffering is a natural part of life that I will embrace. God must love me a lot!

# 7

# Kitty: A Turning Point

As my dad was getting adjusted to prison, my mom and I were also trying to adjust to our new reality. We attended a retreat with Sr. Briege McKenna, who leads a worldwide healing ministry, and we were desperately in need of emotional healing.

Since there were nine hundred women attending the retreat, we were told that there would be no individual prayer ministry with this gifted nun and her prayer companion, Fr. Kevin Scallon. But when Sr. Briege got to the microphone, she said she had asked Jesus that morning what she could do for him that day. His answer was clear.

"Briege, I want you to pray with the women."

"All nine hundred of them, Lord?" she asked incredulously.

"Yes," he replied.

The auditorium erupted in joy as the leaders figured out how they would make this work. When my row came down to the front, I reached my hands out to Jesus in the Eucharist, who was exposed in the monstrance on the altar. Through copious tears, I entrusted my dad and our family to his care, asked him to heal my heart, and rededicated myself to writing and singing for him.

When Sr. Briege and Fr. Kevin got to me, they briefly put their hands on my shoulders and prayed. But when Sr. Briege saw my tears, she gently placed her hand over my cheek and said, "Ohhh." It was as if Jesus himself put his hand on my face that night, and something deep within me was healed.

The next day, in the Adoration chapel, I started writing a song for my dad called "Surrender," and I left that weekend on fire for pursuing music ministry. This song would become very important to my dad and my family. I committed myself to daily prayer, daily Mass, and regular adoration of the Blessed Sacrament. It was a turning point in my life.

# 8

# February 1998

What a difference a month can make! My new world is now fairly well defined. And although it is a far cry from paradise, it is equally distant from the black hole of Kolkata. For my first month, I forced myself to think of my confinement not as prison but as a thirty-day retreat. I prayed, read Scripture, meditated, and cried a lot. Our loving God answered my prayers, not with relief from the courts or an early release but with many small, unexpected gifts, and best of all, a sense of calmness and peace that defies understanding.

Occasionally that peace is interrupted when I get involved in legal wrangling on my case. My isolation and powerlessness are sources of great frustration. However, as soon as I relax and surrender to my fate, the peace returns.

I am going to try having a "mindset of the month." This month FPC (Federal Prison Camp) Pensacola will become an expensive California "fat farm." I will focus on health, diet, exercise, wellness, and prayer. In fact, my life here is much like the Pritikin Center in California, except that I have more freedom than a Pritikin patient, the food is better, and it doesn't cost $5,000 per week.

February 1998

Most of the time, with interruptions now diminishing, I feel spirit-filled and uplifted. Fr. Joe has involved me more in chapel events. Our prayer group is growing slowly, and the men's choir is coming back to life. Often men approach me to wish me well, to express regret about the circumstances that brought me here, and to discuss the inner secrets of their hope or their despair.

## The Insight Program

A handsome, all-American-looking guy told me, with tears in his eyes, that he had spent nine years in prison. He attended the chapel-sponsored "Insights" encounter last weekend, saying that for the first time in nine years, he was "free." Here he choked up and made me promise I would go to the next session, in March. I'm signed up.

The program is controversial among the inmates. As men bare their hearts and souls to each other, many cry publicly for the first time. They are then ridiculed by the macho men, who call the program "Hug-a-Thug." Yet most if not all who attend come away changed for the better, much like Cursillo participants. It's a hopeful program.

My meditation a few days ago focused on the following quote. Sin has four characteristics:

- » self-sufficiency instead of faith
- » self-will instead of submission
- » self-seeking instead of benevolence
- » self-righteousness instead of humility.

All you who know me recognize that I have always felt self-sufficiency was a great virtue, that a strong will was essential for success, that self-seeking was okay as long as the rules of combative fair play were followed, and that self-righteousness was befitting of a high priest (me) in search of justice (courtroom victory). Now fate has forced me to my knees in faith and submission. I seek benevolence and have no choice but humility. This could all be an unexpected blessing. Time will tell.

## Mail

Inmates make bets on how many letters I will receive in a day. Sixteen is the current record. One grumpy guard cursed at the volume of my mail and said out loud, "He must have lots of money these people want." I replied, "I'm a well-known rap star from Baton Rouge." He's not quite sure what the deal is, but he doesn't hassle me anymore.

In my first almost six weeks here, I received 132 letters. Each is precious to me, and I have answered about 120 of them. Previously I felt that personal correspondence was a chore; now I look forward to an hour or two of writing each day, with more on the weekends.

Fr. Frank wrote me a wonderful inspirational letter that referred to 2 Corinthians 12:1-12. This is the same passage shared by another friend a few weeks before my trial and read at Mass the day the jury decided my fate. It seems to be the story of my life.

All will wash out in the end. For St. Paul, the suffering appeared to last four years. And God told him, "My grace is sufficient for you." Paul survived and lived an extraordinary life after prison, achieving true power through total surrender and total trust in God.

FEBRUARY 1998

## Schedule

Today was pretty much routine: 5:30 a.m. wake up; 5:45 get up; 6:15 Scripture and meditation; 6:45 breakfast; 7:00 walk and first daily Rosary; 7:30 report to work.

Then I had 11 a.m. lunch, walk and second Rosary; back to work at 12:15 p.m.; 2:30 p.m. typing class; 3:45-4:00 relax in bunk; 4:00 security "standing" count to prove we are here and not dead; 4:30 supper; 5:00 phone call home (skipped walk due to cold), then reading in bunk; 6:00 Mass at chapel; 7:00-8:00 writing letters; 8:30 men's prayer group and third daily Rosary; 9:30-10:30 reading; and then lights out.

They show one classic movie and two new releases each week. I miss most of the movies and watch no TV. Once a week I read a newspaper. Don't be alarmed about the cost of these extravagances. They are all paid for by what the Navy pays FPC for an inmate's near-slave labor ($5-$20/month) and profits from commissary sales to inmates, which carry a 25-percent markup cost.

Speaking of work, I have a great job: lots of work; lots of praise and gratitude; lots of freedom to move around (in a golf cart, no less); heavy equipment operator's permits (great fun); a large private office with an automatic memory typewriter, microwave oven, coffeepot (for visitors), and unlimited office supplies, plus a VCR. As the official safety program auditor, I have now authored twenty manuals. My favorites include *Haz/Com Standard and OSHA Compliance, Composting at FPC Pensacola, Food Preparation Plans,* and *Ten Commandments of Safety* (I dress up like Moses to lecture on this last one).

I have to say that my pride and joy is the new *Inmate Job Safety Manual*. FPC Pensacola, with 460 slave laborers, only has one "time loss" injury for every thirty-four years of labor. (Maybe this proves that we don't work very long or hard, but we will study that later.)

## Super Bowl

The Super Bowl was a riot here, almost literally. The FPC has three big screen TVs and six regular TVs. Everyone cheered for Denver, the underdog. No bets or pools permitted.

All but I brought huge amounts of food and soft drinks. The "cooking" was incredible but inedible. Groups pooled their resources, dumping nacho chips into giant garbage bags along with a variety of meats, fish, vegetables, dips, and spices. Someone's fingers served to thoroughly mix the ingredients.

The bags were opened, and huge handfuls were scooped onto paper towels covering the tables. Eating without utensils was the norm. I passed on this delicacy, mumbling about a promise I made to St. Jude to fast on each Super Bowl Sunday until the Saints win one.

## Escapes

Anyone who wants to can walk away any day. Three have done so since I've been here, and all were caught quickly. I understand it is usually the Colombian drug dealers with long sentences who "skip."

It's hard on us who stay: lockdowns, restriction to dorms, strip searches, breath alcohol tests, drug tests. I've had them all. They serve as reminders that this is a prison and a significant percentage of the population really wants us to suffer.

February 1998

## Family!

Joey and Caitlin have come on three alternate Sundays to visit. Twice Kitty joined them. Joey and Kitty have sung at the inmate Mass. The inmates love them.

Last Sunday the new inmate choir sang. I'm in it (back row, singing softly). Caitlin joined us at a microphone. She really seems to enjoy the visits. She plays football or jumps rope with other kids, whom she immediately befriends.

There is a bittersweet side effect of visits. They vividly remind me of the life I have lost and may not rejoin for a decade.

Here's my rundown on the girls, youngest to oldest for a change. Caitlin is a joy. Great student! Great athlete! A real trooper. In her basketball games, she has scored well over half her team's points. Yesterday she sank a three-point shot from half court at the buzzer in a close game.

Caroline loves Vanderbilt, has a 3.7 GPA, went on a wilderness campout and hike in the snow, and writes to me every day. Trish is in California, to be close to her boyfriend. She is searching for a job and preparing for the California nursing exam.

Beth writes often, came to visit, and is doing well in her business in New York City. Connie is saving heathen freshmen souls at St. Pius X High School in Atlanta. She sent me seven wonderful spiritual books. Kitty is teaching, singing professionally, and being a good wife and daughter. Her visits here are a sensation.

All the girls are doing Dad-sympathy diets and exercising (to some degree), so that I won't be in better shape than they are.

## Projects

My projects are great diversions:

a. Plowing the playing field starts Monday. What fun!
b. Hug-a-Thug will begin in March.
c. Model planes got preliminary approval, but a committee has to decide if this will look too much like fun.
d. Typing class is going great. It is really soul satisfying to have one's fingers go to the right keys without looking. Look out, Rhonda (my secretary), I'm getting good: twenty to twenty-five words per minute and 98 percent accurate.

## Back at the Dorm

Tim, my first close friend, left last week. I miss him. My roommates voted me his bunk and locker. This was a big deal because he has shelves in his locker, a bottom bunk by a window, and a night light for late reading. Here that's the equivalent of a Windsor Court Presidential Suite. I was really touched when the "palace" was voted to me, since usually this is based on seniority in room residence.

Another roomie left today: a young Colombian cash courier from Bogota. More will go soon. It's so happy for them but so sad for those of us who stay—especially those with long roads to trod till exit day. Mine is October 8, 2006, unless the court of appeals grants relief.

The dorms are noisy and getting noisier for some reason. Language by the loud talkers is an abomination. Fortunately, they are a small minority, with none in my room.

Casino is the big card game here. Bets are in push-ups, sit-ups, and dancing like Michael Jackson. Loser chooses and pays on the spot. It's great fun. Maybe you have to be here to understand.

## Health

Medical care here is lousy to nonexistent. One friend has been in agony with a kidney stone attack for eight days. No help except pain pills. I don't know how he hangs on. Dental appointments take eleven *months* to schedule.

My health is great. Exercise aches and pains are gone. The blisters on my feet from wearing steel-toed boots are healed, and my case of bubonic athlete's foot is responding to intensive care. It's nice to walk without a limp, though prisoners who limp get respect.

My "hair flap" is gone forever. I have a shiny, bald, well-scarred dome, but it doesn't look ridiculous. Weight down twenty pounds at last weigh-in.

In closing, let me assure everyone that your prayers, loyalty, concern, letters, visits, and books are greatly appreciated and will never be forgotten. Thanks for being there for me. You are all in my prayers and thoughts.

# 9

# March 1998

For two full days, wild weather has wreaked havoc at FPC Pensacola. The rain has poured day and night, shutting down all activities except walking to meals in the rain (without rain gear) three times each day.

Our dorm room is a mess. The air hangs stale and heavy from eight men in a small box with no ventilation. Towels hung to dry on the ends of bunks twenty-four hours ago are still wet. It is so dark in the room that I am writing this letter on my bunk to be near a window.

Last night band after a band of thunderstorms roared through with unrelenting lightning and thunder. I decided to leave the window over my bunk open for air, even with rain blowing in. Then lightning hit a tree just outside my window. The tall pine trees at Saufley Field took a beating all night. We will be confined to quarters all day again. It's like being in *prison!*

MARCH 1998

## Thoughts on Suffering

I have lots of time to read, think, and pray here. In the relaxed atmosphere of "snail's-pace-and-proud-of-it" government work, my challenge is no longer day-to-day crisis management. This permits time to focus on faith, the meaning of suffering in life, and the very purpose of human existence. To my amazement, answers are beginning to come to me, bit by bit. At the risk of sounding preachy, I would like to pass along some of my personal musings, for whatever they are worth.

The core question centers on the reason for suffering and death. They are shared by all of us and probably understood by few. We all seem to spend much of our lives searching for security, attempting to avoid suffering, and trying to forget about death. These universal urges are the lure of the dark side.

The great paradox of life, and especially the paradox of a *prosperous* life, is that the more we have accumulated in our search for security and happiness, the more we are doomed to suffer despair and true sorrow, because the search is futile. This is why the search for power, wealth, and possessions is described in the Old Testament as the "vanity of vanities" (Ecclesiastes 1:2).

On the bright side, when we are stripped of all we have devoted our lives to—whether by illness, injury, separation from family and friends, failure, injustice, or prejudice—if we turn to God, we can experience peace, security, contentment, and eventually overwhelming joy. This is the great paradox of suffering. It is in suffering that we find what we have searched for all our lives. Finally we get to "scratch the primal itch" that we all share, the inherent longing for unity with our God.

One personal example may illustrate my point. I have always enjoyed cooking, eating, and drinking. When I arrived here, I had accumulated 268 pounds of dividends from pursuit of these "harmless" pleasures. Something moved me to submit to this disappointment rather than complain. I also chose to give up the few pleasures that could come from salt, sugar, sauces, gravies, salad dressings, fats, breads, desserts, cigars, coffee, and alcohol.

The results are astounding. I am losing three to five pounds a week, I have totally eliminated indigestion from my life, and I am hungry for and thoroughly enjoy every meal.

I am amazed to find more satisfaction in hunger than in being satiated. Less truly is more!

While I seldom see most of you now, this separation has led me to treasure my relationship with each of you more—through interest, focus, correspondence, and concern. Perhaps Caitlin (now nine years old) is better off with a father who is physically absent but no longer distracted, tired, and unfocused on her little life. I am mentally and emotionally tuned in on every bounce of her Biddy League basketball game, every joy and sorrow of her life, and the joy of a few phone calls, letters, and visits each month.

In all this I am beginning to discern meaning and a gospel message. It is *good news* that we all suffer, because it is then that God can prove his faithfulness to us. We are never abandoned. In fact, the more we surrender to God in a spirit of trusting acceptance to what seems a wretched, unjust curse, the more we are rewarded.

We can't mope into the night in self-pity. Our suffering in life and even our death are the path to holiness and to an eternity in heaven. The lonely darkness of Good Friday and the apparent reality of utter destruction signal that the resurrection and the new and better life are near. "Power is made perfect in weakness" (2 Corinthians 12:9).

Lest anyone feel these thoughts are morbid, I want to assure you that I look forward to Sunday brunch at 10 a.m. because of the one weekly treat of boiled eggs and chocolate milk. It is not breakfast at Brennan's, but I will enjoy it as much or more than Eggs Benedict and Café Brûlot, without any side effects.

A final thought: the Scripture readings for Mass on Sunday, February 15, reiterated the theme that God reveals himself in our suffering if we turn to him. Prosperity that distracts us from God is a curse, not a blessing. Madison Avenue preaches that happiness and contentment are found in power, self-centeredness, and wealth. But our envied prosperity is like a millstone around our collective necks.

Thank God that he permits us to suffer, as it leads us to an understanding of both life and death.

## Deacon Duties and Other Interests

There is an unfortunate BOP regulation that prohibits any inmate from engaging in ordained ministry. (I'm told this was done to muzzle a prominent preacher during his confinement.) After I requested a variance from the warden, she only approved what the chaplain would agree to be "unordained" ministry.

At this time, we do not have even one Lenten service, devotion, program, or talk. I hear that we might be permitted to have a Way of the Cross on Good Friday.

I am taking a new class on parenting. It focuses on absentee parenting and security issues for children when their dad is away. To my surprise, I am the only white student; all the rest are young black men. I don't believe any are actually married to their children's mothers.

These guys have to deal with layers of problems in their lives, starting with poverty and ignorance (not stupidity). My life and family relations seem utopian by comparison. They all share a genuine interest in their kids and a desire to make their lives better.

I'm still walking, stretching, lifting, and going to abs class fanatically. My condition is rapidly improving. Most of my sore muscles and joints have healed since being rudely forced out of retirement ten weeks ago. I couldn't even see my toes at that point, and now I can touch them with the palm of my hand! Even my bad knee feels like new, and my back and shoulder pain have all but disappeared.

If I could write the prison wellness book and talk people into spending six months doing what I am at least partially being forced to do, I could change the way Americans feel and act. I could get rich besides (though this is no longer a personal goal). The problem is that I could never talk anyone into the bland diet, spiritual exercises, TV and newspaper ban, incoming phone call block, and uncluttered life I get free of charge courtesy of the BOP. We rarely do what's really good for us voluntarily, do we?

## Friends

There is a real sense of loss here when roommates leave. Three of mine left recently. In discussing this with seasoned inmates, I learned that most men here consciously avoid developing close friendships because the pain of separation is so acute. And the pain of imprisonment is so pronounced that most inmates never look back after release. They don't write or visit their former roommates, no matter how many promises they have made. They simply can't do it.

## MARCH 1998

One inmate whom I like and talk to a good deal (another mid-fifties lawyer) so attempted to keep me at a distance with curmudgeon-like rudeness that I was concerned. When I asked if I had unintentionally offended him, he was surprised. This old dog then told me with tears in his eyes that his long sentence meant he would always be the one left behind, and he simply couldn't bear the pain of repeated separations. He has warmed up some, now that he knows I have the longest sentence of anyone here.

For almost all visitors, the reality of my life has been sad but also reassuring. I'm in no danger, but I am confined and dehumanized by the system in many subtle and some not-so-subtle ways. Life's basic lessons of faith, perseverance, gratitude, hope, patience, and joy are easier for me to master here, where I am totally powerless and substantially isolated, than they were as an all-out litigator in the middle of things.

After I return home, I hope I can look back on all that has happened as a great learning experience. Keep me in your prayers, please.

# 10

# April 1998

I had some physically and emotionally difficult days this past month. I was suffering from heat exhaustion and was also reprimanded for various minor "infractions" that were not infractions at all. The powers that be threatened me with solitary confinement or worse: being shipped off to another prison! Even with all of that, there were some bright spots.

During our Toastmasters meeting, I was asked to evaluate a young, nice-looking guy who seemed painfully shy and ill at ease. Early on I decided that I would only make positive and encouraging comments about his speech. He then gave one of the most moving talks I have ever heard.

Eduardo explained that he was one of many children in an impoverished Puerto Rican family. He didn't know his father, and by the time he was eight years old, his mother put him out because she couldn't afford to take care of him. As a full-time street child, he lived in terror much of the time.

In the horror of his struggle to survive, there was one bright spot: his best and only friend. They did everything together and took care of each other. By the time they were eleven years old, they were able to survive.

Then Eduardo's friend committed suicide. Eduardo passionately described the impact of that event. No one cared about the death of an eleven-year-old street child. Eduardo said simply that the bullet that took his only friend's life killed two people. Eduardo's statement was in fact true. Except for his beating heart, he too was dead.

Then, smiling broadly, Eduardo said that being imprisoned was, without a doubt, the best experience of his life. He gave no further explanation at the time. When he concluded his talk, a hush fell over the room as every person was moved to tears, something not often seen in public here.

Later I asked Eduardo why going to prison was such a great experience for him. (I think that my experience is not so great.) He patiently explained that he had been brought back to life by the Insight program. I'm glad I signed up for this.

## Work News

I am still writing manuals when not grading roads or plowing the ball fields. Next week my cohort Paul (a former New Orleans banker) and I will start teaching the janitors how to clean toilet bowls, showers, and urinals. Safety work involves lots of glamour, which Paul and I enjoy.

My pay has been increased from the lowest hourly rate to the second highest, from three to twenty-nine cents an hour. At this rate I will go home rich!

The most ambitious project by far is rewriting the *Admission and Orientation Manual*. Drunk with power, I have made it a capital offense to make noise or to shout street corner profanity within earshot of my room. If the dorm rules are adopted and enforced, 99 percent of the inmates will be ecstatic.

## "I Will Never Forget You."

During the fourth week of Lent, I found great consolation in several passages from Scripture assigned for Mass. The first, from Isaiah 49, promises that "on the day of salvation" the prisoners will be told to come out, and their days of suffering will be replaced with restful waters and level highways through the mountains (49:9). Isaiah promises that God will comfort the afflicted who feel that they have been forsaken. The passage concludes with

> Can a mother forget her infant,
> be without tenderness for the child of her womb?
> Even should she forget,
> I will never forget you. (49:15)

Two days later the reading was from the Book of Wisdom. The author reflects on the evil done to innocent people by pious and self-righteous hypocrites. The passage describes how just people are obnoxious to the wicked. This particularly includes the wicked who style themselves as children of God. They scheme to test the belief that God cares for and protects those who are faithful to him. They test the just man's patience and gentleness with revilement and torture.

> These were their thoughts, but they erred,
> for their wickedness blinded them,
> And they did not know the hidden counsels of God;

> neither did they count on a recompense of holiness,
> nor discern the innocent souls' reward. (2:21-22)

The next day this theme was renewed in passages from Jeremiah, who was trustingly led to the slaughter that had been plotted for him. The plotters intended to "cut him off from the land of the living, so that his name will no longer be remembered" (11:19).

At times I feel that this has been done to me, too. Like Jeremiah, I seek to entrust my cause to our loving God, hoping that in due time I will be restored and justice will prevail. At times it is difficult to believe, as even my memory of who I am begins to fade.

## Hug-a-Thug

Exactly a week after the reading from Jeremiah, the Insight program began. I had no idea what to expect. In the opening session, it became evident that the team consisted of forty inmates who had participated in earlier weekends, plus a civilian staff of three psychologists. Twenty new recruits sat nervously in a quiet isolation room, anticipating what was to come. Men with shaved heads, ponytails, ugly purple scars, and nightmarish tattoos exchanged rough talk, posturing, and profanity. Everyone seemed inordinately nervous.

The next thirty hours were controlled pandemonium. We had a series of sharing and communication exercises. I heard stories of personal tragedy and suffering that left me stunned. This unusual group was in tears of shared sadness and suffering. I've never seen anything like it before, except perhaps on a Cursillo weekend.

Then came a transformation to wild celebration and hysterical laughter, as inmate skits were used to lift the heavy mood. Incidentally, I wrote, produced, and directed the comedy skit put on by my group of ten inmates. It was both fun and funny.

Because of the agreement of strict confidentiality, I will not repeat even generically any of the stories that the men shared with each other. It was a great healing experience premised on faith in our loving God and unconditional support, affection, and love from our fellow human beings and friends.

My great problem here has been a feeling of loneliness and isolation. I seldom let my guard down. Now there are at least a hundred other men who have shared the Insight experience. Most if not all have been transformed by it. Wherever I go now, I am greeted by name with a warm smile and words of simple encouragement. I know that no matter how long I am here, I will never again feel lonely and isolated.

This program is effective, unlikely, emotional, and interesting in an environment where dehumanization seems to be the norm. I plan to help put on the next event in about three months.

In closing, I wish to assure all of you that I am at peace, even in the dark hours. Each day brings new insights and adventures of the spirit. After only three-and-a-half months, it's hard to believe that there is anything left to experience.

Thank you sincerely for your kindnesses and prayers.

---

> Encourage souls to place great trust in My fathomless mercy. Let the weak, sinful soul have no fear to approach Me, for even if it had more sins than there are grains of sand in the world, all would be drowned in the unmeasurable depths of My mercy. (*Diary*, 1059)

---

# 11

# MAY 1998

On Easter weekend, Joey and five of the girls came to visit. They all sang with the inmate choir at Easter Sunday Mass. As a Communion meditation, they sang "Refiner's Fire" together, a special song they had rehearsed before they came. It was positively angelic.

Many of the inmates had tears in their eyes. Dozens came to me later to say how much they were touched by the beautifully blended sound of the sisters plus Mom. One man told Kitty it was the first tears of joy he had shed in six years.

## Patience

My most obviously lacking virtue is patience. I have spent my entire life avoiding lines, moving purposefully in high gear. So one positive impact of my confinement is that I am finally learning to be patient. I've had no choice.

For example, an appointment for nonemergency dental work can be scheduled *one year* from now! If I had an emergency, I could see the dentist in about three months. After getting an appointment, the wait in the hallway (with no chairs) can take from early morning to mid-afternoon.

Lines for meals can take half an hour. There are always lines to get a washer or a dryer. Wednesday's laundry might not actually get done until Friday.

Shopping is maddening. The commissary is open one hour per week for "major purchases." This means that all 450 inmates show up at the commissary window at the same time, and delays for the simplest purchase often run over an hour.

There are lines for the phones each night; lines in the mess hall for turning in platters, plates, and trays; long lines to see a case counselor and to try to get mail. At "rush hour," there are even lines for bathroom stalls and showers. Getting work equipment takes days, and then finding someone with access to fuel is always a hassle.

With this much pressure on a compulsively hurried person, it was sure to happen sooner or later: I collapsed into a whimpering pile of patience. I knew the breakdown was complete when it took me well over an hour to eat a bag of plain M&M's. Without thinking, I ate them one at a time, letting each individual piece melt without chewing it.

Now I carry a book in my pocket. When the lines queue up, I simply read until the wait is over. I no longer start my stopwatch to see if the delay will set a new record.

## New Stuff

We recently received gym lockers from some other government facility. They are twice the size of our old ones. I now have space for everything I own, including my pressed uniforms. I look like the inmate from *GQ* magazine.

MAY 1998

The back of my locker door is covered with photographs that family and friends have been kind enough to send. The lockers, refreshed with a coat of battleship gray paint, complement the off-white walls and floor. Our room is now a model of institutional good taste.

The ball field and track-leveling project was so successful that the warden ordered that a real track be built, with a clay base and crushed gray cinders as a surface. I took on the project with enthusiasm. I had a dump truck lined up to haul away the old dirt. Then I was going to put in a clay base with a cinder top layer.

Unfortunately, the front-end loader blew up just before I was to start work. This weekend the head mechanic from the naval base, who is a friend from my abs class, will try to fix it.

I was drafted as an unrestricted free agent to play on the Grumpy Old Men, last year's champion Over-40 Softball team. I'll give it a try until something breaks, tears, or collapses. My average after two preseason games is a team-leading .750. But I have trouble hitting the slow-pitch balls.

## *The Dark Night of the Soul*

This work of the mystic St. John of the Cross aptly describes my state of mind. St. John wrote while he was unjustly imprisoned, during the time of the Reformation. So far I believe he is saying that to find God in our lives, we must deliberately encounter and embrace the "dark night of the soul." That is, we must intentionally release everything we love in this world.

This doesn't sound like much fun. In prison, 90 percent of the surrender and release takes place involuntarily. John promises great rewards after the detachment process of the dark night is successfully accomplished. If I can get there, I will surely let all of you know if it is worth the trouble, loneliness, and pain of separation. It certainly puts a unique spin on becoming a federal prisoner.

Saturday night one of my roommates was caught in an escape attempt. I believe he was just leaving for a date, but he was "cuffed and shipped" immediately. It was sad to see him crying as he left. Apparently this guy had been leaving regularly and talked freely of his exploits. One of his "buddies" snitched on him.

My Beginner Abs Class certificate just came in. I'm now officially an intermediate (five hundred crunches per session) after more than four months of hell. Most of the old aches and pains are gone, but softball has brought bruised fingers and sore legs. My weight loss is now between forty-five and fifty pounds and slowing some. I may start jogging soon!

I absolutely cherish the letters I receive. I've lost count after passing five hundred. Write if you can, but please don't feel guilty if you can't. Time is flying by for me now, and I hope to be home by year's end.

# 12

# June 1998

It's hard for me to believe that I've been here for almost six months. My Fifth Circuit Court of Appeals brief will be filed on June 19. Optimism is high for a reversal. In the meantime, the adventure of living here continues.

I have been asked to write a monthly column for the *Kenner Star*. The column will feature nondenominational Scripture analysis and interpretation for practical use in everyday living. My first reaction was to decline since I know little about Scripture, and interpretation and application are so varied and personal. But as I thought about the idea, I realized that Scripture reflection has taken on a new meaning for me.

My old impression of Scripture as an ambiguous, cryptic, and sterile collection of pious-but-impractical platitudes has changed. Now I see messages of hope, consolation, and encouragement. Scripture is like a vast, verdant pasture with endless waves of knee-high, brilliant green grass. And I see myself as a peacefully grazing old bull whose mission is to live with contentment and appreciation while exploring the vast plain.

I have surrendered to total dependence on our loving God, with delusions of personal power shattered. God is the center of meaning in the universe, and I sit peacefully in his presence. I feel a new sense of innocence, simplicity, and trust, in contrast to my former life of self-deception and avoidance of life's difficult issues.

Many solutions are tried in the search for security: power, wealth, success, fame, beauty, and self-realization are a few. Here the solution is simple: faith and Scripture. So I will write about my journey and experiences in the hope that it will make sense to others.

## New Crises

Wouldn't you know it! My dorm room is being converted into a Spanish-language TV room, and we all must find new places to live. We will lose our room seniority, bottom bunks, night lights, and windows. Our diverse group gets along so well, and we hate to start over with new roommates.

Rumor has it that I will be moved into the infamous "cave" of Big Mississippi. His room has plenty of vacant bunks because he snores like a freight train, breaks wind like a bull elephant, and shouts in his sleep. This is not good. For now my strategy is to stall. God must have a sense of humor.

Oh, and there are criminals here! This week I left my laundry unattended, and my treasured light-gray, all-cotton T-shirt disappeared. It may not sound like much, but the shirt was 50 percent of my private wardrobe, and this item is no longer available in the commissary. My kingdom for an indelible laundry marker.

JUNE 1998

## Better News

The Grumpy Old Men led the Over-40 Softball league! Amazingly, my batting average is now somewhere around .800. In Sunday's stunning win, 20-6 over the second-place team, I was three for three!

Toastmasters is a weekly highlight. I gave a speech entitled "Funereal Fun." I told several of my best funeral stories, after pointing out that the word "funeral" begins with the word "fun." When I finished, the toastmaster assured me that all were eagerly looking forward to my funeral and all the fun that would be had on that auspicious occasion.

At one meeting, we had about ten visitors from the Pensacola club. It was one of the occasions during which we were allowed to talk to "regular" people. Mrs. Joy was a last-minute speaker. Her impromptu speech included vivid memories from her childhood. We laughed, cried, and cheered wildly. She won the blue ribbon that night, and I hope Mrs. Joy will return.

## Departures

It is a truly bittersweet event when an inmate friend is released or transferred. This month there were three: "Laundry Joe" (who ran the laundry), "Two Scoop" Lou (the mess hall soft-serve ice cream man), and "Little Art" (the camp carpenter/cabinet/furniture maker) who was our reader at Mass.

The going-away party featured cigars for all, a disgusting homemade cake from an unknown source, and a wastebasket full of fresh fruit ambrosia. The invitation-only event was held in the visiting yard, and the prison stories flowed at flood level. Good luck, guys!

## More on *The Dark Night of the Soul*

This book is slow going, partially because it was written in Spanish over four hundred years ago but also because the concepts are difficult. The first third of the journey is separation from the vast array of human appetites that consume our consciousness, energy, and time. Not an easy process without outside compulsion (like being a prisoner).

The second step is even more difficult: the step of faith. This is an almost mystical willingness to completely surrender to the search for God and the guidance of his Spirit. St. John makes an interesting point about this step. It is the darkest part of the process, because its experiences surpass description in human terms. His illustrations of the point are interesting.

First, imagine the brightest manmade light. At night it is so brilliant that it is blinding, but at noon on a bright clear day, the sunlight overwhelms it. Human comprehension is similarly overwhelmed when we place ourselves in the presence of God through simple faith.

According to St. John, describing this is like trying to describe a brilliant color to a person blind from birth. Since the person has no frame of reference, the description is impossible. This period of frustration is the darkest part of the dark night of the soul. I think I'm there now.

## Fun Stuff

I have made friends with a Cubano whose family made cigars on a large plantation in Cuba. He explained to me the time and effort that go into the formidable process—from perfect seed selection to planting to harvest to production. When I got a note pad and

## June 1998

pen and asked to be retold the process and terminology so that I could give a Toastmasters talk on cigars, his face clouded, and he politely declined. He explained that his family would never forgive him if they heard that he had revealed their secrets to a gringo.

A friend sent me a copy of Lincoln's biography, which was quite a revelation. In many of his efforts, he was a total failure. This included business, politics, law, and his personal life. The obvious secrets to his successes were persistence, humor, colorful little stories, and passionate belief in the causes he advocated. He was little good with technical defenses for the guilty and undeserving, but a tiger in the defense of the innocent and powerless.

My weight hit a new low, and I can do between seven and eight hundred crunches. My new treat each week is a soft-serve ice cream topped with three scoops of chocolate sauce, crushed Oreo cookies, and chopped peanuts. After many months of "no-frills" dining, I almost went into shock from all the sugar.

I'm sure St. John of the Cross would understand. As I type, the struggle with my conscience has started. Since I'm drooling on the keyboard, I can predict that there will be another ice cream treat tonight.

I'm helping organize a Father's Day party for the inmates' kids. We will have traditional favorites like "pin the tie on the dad," water balloon toss to—and at—dads, hopscotch, dodgeball, and horse races. Guess who the horses will be, on all fours. There will be snacks, coloring, sack races, bat spins, and much more.

The idea is to actually get the dads and kids to play together for a few carefree hours. The big unknown is heat. I suggested that we hook up the fire hose and spray everyone from time to time. Should be fun.

The many visits and hundreds of letters that I receive are the lifelines that connect me to the life and reality that I once had and hope to return to soon. Your kindness and thoughtfulness will never be forgotten and can never be repaid. May God bless you all.

# 13

# July 1998

On Monday, June 29, I celebrated six months as Federal Inmate 25306-034. What a milestone! Never in my wildest imagination did I anticipate this "passage" in my life. I have survived and prospered in all ways (except financial) to a degree that is surprising. I am relaxed, calm, peaceful, rested, healthy, and adjusted to a life that I never knew existed.

Now I am sure that I can hold on until my appeal is decided. That process moves slowly, but I have learned to think in terms of months instead of minutes. So if anyone has been feeling sorry for me or worrying about how I am really, desist.

If the appeal is successful, there will be a great homecoming celebration around or after Christmas, and you are all invited. If I lose, I hope to find the strength to endure cheerfully. Now on to new fun in the sun, BOP style.

## Abbreviations and Terms

Several people have asked about abbreviations that recur in my monthly epistles. The following are a few of the essential prison terms.

***BOP: Bureau of Prisons.*** This is the fastest-growing segment of the government bureaucracy. Federal crimes have mushroomed from the two described in the Constitution to more than ten thousand as of 1998. Prisons are expanding at a 30-percent compound annual growth rate, even with crime rates declining.

This new growth industry has been named the prison industrial complex. The USA proudly boasts a larger percentage of its population behind bars than any other country in the world.

***FPC: Federal Prison Camp.*** I'm in FPC Pensacola.

***HACK: Hard Ass Carrying Keys.*** This is the term of endearment used by inmates to refer to their "keepers." Since the guards are not permitted to carry weapons of any kind, status is determined by the size and weight of one's key chain. The more keys and the bigger the keys, the greater the status.

Officially these are "correctional officers." Their mission is to reform inmates through close and benevolent supervision while maintaining order in the institution. Entering this noble profession requires no education, no experience, and no written tests. Salaries are low, but benefits are good. Job security is absolute, with civil service and a union. Power over hapless inmates is absolute, unless there is an impartial witness.

Some hacks are palpably human. Some are perversely evil and mean. Most are simply indifferent.

***Abs.*** This is an abbreviation for abdominal muscles. The abs class is actually part aerobics, lots of stretching and body contortions, and then seven to eight hundred abdominal crunches. After six months of serious pain and effort, I can now do the routine without cheating too much.

Abs class looks easy from a distance, but it definitely is not. Enduring this class on Mondays, Thursdays, and Saturdays makes strip searches, waiting in line, and dehumanization almost pleasant by comparison. I now understand that to fully enjoy life's day-to-day pleasures, we must have something to dread. Abs class serves that purpose.

***Short/Long:*** This sometimes derisive term is used to describe how close an inmate is to leaving prison. Certain characteristics go with being "long" or "short." "Long" inmates are often surly, disagreeable, and grumpy because they are so far from freedom. "Short" inmates fluctuate between ecstasy and shell shock. The joy of freedom is juxtaposed with the harsh reality of the need to get a job, avoid drugs, take responsibility, and provide for personal and family needs.

***Callout.*** No, Mardi Gras fans, this is not an invitation to dance at a carnival ball. This is a daily computer printout that each inmate must check for scheduled appointments and for assignments other than regular work details.

***Down.*** This is not a description of the prototypical inmate's mood. It is used to describe how long an inmate has been a guest of the BOP. I have been "down" for six and a half months. Being down for a long time brings status—at least in the eyes of some inmates.

## The Zoo

My new room is nicknamed The Zoo. As reluctant as I was to move, this place is way quieter than the Bedlam Palace I was in. The interesting inhabitants of The Zoo make up for the practically nonexistent air conditioning and other lost perks, such as my bottom bunk, window, and reading light. The Zoo roster:

***Bunk #1 (top):*** This is mine, complete with a sign featuring the cartoon character Dilbert saying, "Yes, Dilbert, this is where you live now."

***Bunk #1 (bottom):*** Roberto, aka Beto, Mex-Mech, Mex-Mouth, and Chingawa. Beto is short, dark, and constantly chattering, and he has an irrepressible smile and limitless good humor. He never knew his father and has been on his own since he was twelve years old. By his mid-teens he was a drug addict and abused alcohol.

With little formal education, Roberto reads and speaks Spanish and English well. I suspect that his native intelligence is high. He is a gifted mechanic. He has had only a handful of visitors and seldom receives any mail.

Beto is devoutly Catholic. He attends Mass and prays fervently (but secretly) each morning and night. He has religious tattoos on his chest, back, and arms. Every time he takes his shirt off, I feel the urge to light a votive candle.

Beto's stories keep us in hysterics. He can mimic anything and anyone, even inanimate objects and sounds. He leaps around the room, becoming each character in the story.

If I were king, I would send Beto to MIT for an engineering degree and an MBA. He would revolutionize industrial development in Mexico. Instead he will struggle to get a job in a junkyard salvaging used auto parts.

***Bunk #2 (top):*** Bubba is a fortyish white guy from Florida. He is undereducated, rural, and skilled at hunting and fishing (at night, out of season, and without licenses). Bubba has a pot belly that is his pride and joy, black shaggy hair, and a beard and mustache combo right out of Dickens. While I was losing weight, Bubba and I forged a fast friendship, as I gave him all my unwanted food, including the much-prized greasy fried chicken that is served weekly.

Bubba will return to his former job as a part-time roofer when he is released this fall. He is divorced and sees loose, predatory women as the great burden of his life. He has a beautiful teenage daughter who probably favors her mother.

***Bunk #2 (bottom):*** Andrew, a former banker/businessman, now lives at FPC Pensacola for over-reporting his income. His case made it to the US Supreme Court and is still active. In what I have heard and read about his case, he is here because of poor representation.

Andrew is about fifty. His gray hair and beard make him a Kenny Rogers look-alike. He is pleasant, positive, friendly and most importantly, the softball coach of the Grumpy Old Men. Everyone wants to be on his team because he is relaxed and has the unique idea that we play softball for fun. He never yells at his players, and he speaks only for encouragement, not criticism. His efforts to get everyone to relax and have fun result in a close-knit team that wins the close ones.

When released, Andrew plans to syndicate the acquisition of an eighty-thousand-acre ranch in Oregon. I have already been invited out to elk hunt.

***Bunk #3 (top).*** Tommy is a mid-twenties recent FSU Law School graduate, serving time for drug charges. He is quiet, short, crew cut, and totally absorbed in the autobiographical novel he is writing. The novel tells the story of an innocent young man seduced by an evil older woman into a life of degenerate sex and drugs. I have been asked to proofread and edit the manuscript, which has been rewritten seven times by his devoted mother.

To date I have turned down the editing offer. I suspect that the book will be tragically sad and painfully depressing. Although writing is probably good therapy for Tommy, I'm not sure I'm ready to take on his burdens.

***Bunk #3 (bottom):*** William ("Grumpy"), a fiftyish former bank officer from New York, is one of my favorites. He is the camp curmudgeon who sourly complains about everything. Grumpy was initially on my case because he saw me as what he hates most: positive, cheerful, and friendly. He is bitter about being impoverished by a long court battle and receiving a long sentence, while vehemently maintaining his innocence. His case also went to the US Supreme Court.

Grumpy is divorced and never speaks of wife, family, or post-release plans. Beneath the gruff exterior, he is actually sensitive, funny, friendly, and intelligent. He is one of the inmates whom I genuinely like and trust. He knows everyone and everything necessary to get along in prison. He has shunned the Insight program, but he sneaks into Mass when Joey and the girls come to sing.

***Bunk #4 (top):*** Rodrigo is a short, burly, and ominous-looking Mexican drug trafficker. His age is hard to guess but is probably around twenty. He is very quiet and may have some language problems. Two passions occupy his waking hours—dorm cooking and his teenage girlfriend. He writes her daily, and she responds with letters in envelopes covered with Valentine artwork.

Rodrigo seldom has anything to say. I've seen his innocuous smile turn into a menacing glare at the slightest real or imagined slight. He has become friendlier since I gave him a few good cigars. He even offered me some of his "handmade" Mexican snacks.

"Handmade" literally means "made with hands only." No plates, cups, or utensils are used to prepare, serve, or eat the grub. I have developed the digestive system of a desert vulture. To think I used to shun Manuel's Hot Tamales in New Orleans!

**Bunk #4 (bottom):** Miguel is a late forties/early fifties former member of the Mexican Mafia. He is rock hard, both physically and mentally. His glare can bend steel at six paces.

Miguel and Beto both play for the Grumpy Old Men. In an early practice, Miguel tried playing shortstop. Repeatedly the hard-hit balls struck him in the face, arms, legs, and chest. He was bleeding profusely, purple and swollen, with the stitching on the balls clearly imprinted in his skin. If Andrew hadn't insisted that he go to the infirmary for first aid, he would have played without a whimper until he lost consciousness.

Miguel and I went to Insight together. He was utterly transformed from an angry, bitter, violent enforcer for the Mexican Mafia into a peaceful, humble, and penitent man, determined to reestablish his relationship with the wife and children he abandoned. I have heard him say he does not deserve the new beginning that his family has offered him.

Miguel has written lyrics for songs about his life and newly discovered faith. Kitty put one to music for him and sang it at Mass on the Fourth of July weekend. The song was beautiful and the lyrics inspirational (about a simple man and his simple faith). Miguel glowed when he heard the song for the first time. I'm sure Kitty will be getting more lyrics.

After Insight, Miguel reconciled with his wife, from whom he had been estranged for sixteen years. His life of solitude has been replaced with frequent visitors and tearful reunions. He and his wife will remarry when he is released.

## Grazing the Greener Pastures

My first column in the *Kenner Star* was published the first week of July. Writing a column on Scripture has been a challenge. I decided to write about the thoughts that have been the most important to me since I've been here. The challenge is to be literate, scholarly, nondenominational, inspirational, interesting, and practical—in five hundred words or less.

There is a close connection between Scripture and prisoners, since much of it was written by prisoners. As Terry Anderson, the seven-year hostage in Beirut, wrote in his book *Den of Lions*, prison brings a total surrender that puts Scripture in a new and different light. As long as we feel that we have the personal power to run the show, much of the "less is more" paradox of Scripture is lost on us. My column is called "Faithwalk."

As for my appeal, 260 pages of coordinated defense briefs have hit the US attorneys like a preemptive nuclear strike. They are requesting long delays for responding. A thirty-day extension may be granted, but I hope not much more. We are on track now for oral argument this fall. Here's hoping and praying.

The Grumpy Old Men won the regular season and the July Fourth One-Pitch Tournament. Saturday we play the finals of the season-end tournament. A victory brings each member two six-packs of soft drinks. We are out of storage space with all the victories.

Several times in June and early July, Joey and the girls came to sing with the inmate choir. The inmates loved it, and Mass on Sunday was packed. The program for Mass now identifies *The Von Cleveland Family Singers* as such. Even little Caitlin steps up to a microphone.

JULY 1998

Sometimes Kitty's husband, Mel, brings his clarinet and saxophone, and my mother-in-law plays the piano. I enjoy these events more than anything else that happens here.

# 14

# August 1998

This has been one of the most difficult months for me here. Joey and the girls were in Georgia and California for several weeks, so my weekends included fewer visits. Things have been in more turmoil than normal here due to staff changes. We have been living in a state of carefully orchestrated terror. Not a fear of physical violence, but constant uneasiness and concern about just what is going on and how we will be affected. Each time the intercom comes on, everyone tenses up and listens for their name. The staff are all on edge about being moved or eliminated, and no one seems to know what is really going on. I have resolved to stop being nervous about what is going on and to become invisible.

My recent evaluation overlooked 99 percent of my regular activities. It established a "goal" for the next six months of joining Toastmasters. This seems strange since I am the vice-president of Toastmasters and have won several speech contests.

On the outside chance that my activities might positively impact my prospects for leaving here, I submitted a supplement to my Program Review Report. My first effort was rejected unless

I could get verification from my boss that I had really done what I claimed to have done. He will gladly do so, but it's troubling to note that they expect me to lie about my official record.

I did not challenge the staff's conclusion that I have "no problems or concerns" with the prison. It isn't brutal here, but I bet I could come up with one or two "problems or concerns" if I tried.

## Appeal Schedule

The best guess from the Washington attorneys is that there will be a decision in December, January, or February. The government brief is due to be filed by September 10. We have two weeks to reply. Then the oral argument will be set for October or November. I am hoping for the best and have gotten lots of positive feedback from attorneys and others who have read the briefs.

Twenty-six major issues have been raised. Any issue to which the appellate court agrees with us will result in at least a new trial. It could lead to an outright dismissal of the charges against me.

## On a Lighter Note

I noticed the soccer league's Over-40 team rosters recently and thought you would enjoy hearing the names posted: Control Man Harold, Henry the Nigerian Hulk, Locomotive Caicedo, Crazy Legs Gandy, Gato the Professor, Sweet-Cheeks Balsero, Pretty-Boy Manny, Chino Angel, Richard the Sherman Tank, Bloody Mancour, Slowpo Jimenez, Perla the Flame, and Romero the Ugly.

There have been lots of fun visitors in the last few weeks. Each time Kitty comes, the inmates are moved to tears by her beautiful solos and her duets with Joey. I'm becoming known as the "Mass singer's father." Many non-Catholics come just for the music.

My roommates have become aware that I am writing a monthly column about Scripture. Their reactions have been interesting. Most of them are "sneak" Scripture readers and prayers. Few go to church. Most are Protestant, with strong opinions that they vigorously defend. I bounce my ideas off this bunch before writing each Faithwalk column.

## Beto's Remedy

A few weeks ago, I woke up with a severe sore throat that rapidly got worse. Instead of going to the infirmary, I submitted to the herbal cure of Dr. Beto. For a couple days, I drank a concoction of chicken soup with his secret ingredients, including aspirin, herbs, and five or six varieties of peppers from the greenhouse and commissary cans. The concoction was hotter than Tabasco.

After two days, I couldn't stand the cure anymore and declared a complete recovery. Beto was smugly proud, and many others sought his secret recipe.

A few days later, Beto was handcuffed and shipped quickly and quietly to some new facility. His offense was allegedly trying to send out a Father's Day gift that he had made out of scraps of wood and engraved metal through the Navy mail. He will lose his halfway-house eligibility but should still be released this fall. I will probably never hear from him again, but I will never forget his kindness, humor, or spirit.

Nor will I ever encounter such a resourceful mechanic. This probably means that our air conditioner will never work properly again. I will truly miss Beto.

My latest job has been to write and illustrate, with my Picasso-like drawings, a manual for welding. Our real expert, who worked as a welder in Pascagoula, Mississippi, was shipped out for operating a tattoo parlor in the welding shop. Now I am on my own.

Fortunately, just before Beto shipped out, he took me for a tour of the shop and explained what everything is. Our equipment is first rate, and Beto even found the manufacturers' manuals for me to study. So I am now a welder and the resident expert.

## Softball World Series

The Grumpy Old Men won the regular season and the July Fourth tournament. It's the first time I can remember not being the underdog. Everyone was pulling against us in the World Series. We lost that in a hard-fought battle of errors and arguments.

There was some victory even in defeat. Our unprecedented victory streak up to that point won six-packs of soft drinks for each team member. Since I don't drink soft drinks, all my roomies became especially friendly toward me.

## Food for Thought

Denise is a dear friend from the Handicapped Encounter Christ retreats that my wife and I used to help run. Denise has cerebral palsy, is legally blind, can't dress or feed herself, and has difficulty walking and talking. But she has a great mind and, more importantly, the heart of a lion. She is now in her late twenties, has a University of New Orleans master's degree in counseling, and works with the handicapped.

Denise writes to me using a special typewriter. A recent letter arrived on a day when I was down in the dumps and feeling sorry for myself. Denise explained that she had been thinking about me when one of her charges engaged her:

"I was doing some filing when Darrin, one of my rugrats, wheeled himself over to me. Darrin is twenty-nine years old, unable to speak, has never been to school, and is considered 'retarded' by professionals. Darrin talks in charades. He began tugging at my arm to get my attention. When I looked up, he asked why I looked so sad that day.

"I told him about you, what had happened to you, and my sad dream about you the night before. I went back to my files, and I thought Darrin had gone back to his computer game. After a few minutes, I felt another tug on my arm. Somewhat impatiently, I looked up. Darrin was waving his arms, trying to say something.

"After ten minutes, I was able to translate. He wanted me to know that he would pray for my friend every day; not to worry, that my friend would be OK, and that God would bring my friend back to us in time. I thanked him, not only for myself but for you, Joey, the girls, and all who have traveled this painful journey with you."

As I read Denise's letter, my mopey self-pity evaporated. I was overwhelmed with the thought that Darrin was selflessly praying for me when it would seem appropriate for us to reverse roles. I will someday go home. In the meantime, I am blessed with good health, education, personal resources, and a large, active support group of family and friends. Darrin is serving a life sentence in a prison created by a body that doesn't work and from which he cannot escape.

Here's a heartfelt thanks to the dynamic double Ds—Denise and Darrin—for their thoughtfulness, kindness, prayers, and good example.

# 15

# SEPTEMBER 1998

Other than a close brush with Hurricane Earl, things have been quiet and pretty much routine. I have become a model prisoner. I am actually the same as always, but now, no matter what happens, I try to give a cheerful and patient response. I've learned that patience is a virtue, and I am repeating the remedial course.

As I was meditating on the subject of prayer, a new thought kept reappearing: "Dear God, please let me go home." That pretty much sums up where I am spiritually. Although I am miraculously at peace and time seems to fly, I am developing a deep yearning for home and the mundane experiences that I took for granted for so long. If this prayer is answered in an affirmative way, I will return home a much different person.

### Achievement Man

Some member of the Zoo saw my note from the warden complimenting me on my "many accomplishments" here. So I now have the nickname "Achievement Man." It came with a monogrammed costume made out of a set of Big Mississippi's underwear, stolen by a fearless inmate. The teasing has escalated to include public singing of the Achievement Man theme song, sung to the tune of Mighty Mouse: "Here he comes to save the day. Achievement Man is on the way!" This can be embarrassing when it happens at a softball game.

I was assigned to figure out how to safely operate the prison steam cleaner, which no one had operated for years because the manual was lost. Using the trial-and-*many*-errors method, I eventually had the boiler roaring and several guys running for cover. All machines that make lots of noise and smoke are truly soul satisfying.

# 16

## OCTOBER 1998

The last thirty days have been more than interesting in some new ways. We have had Hurricane Georges, the departure of several of the inmates I considered to be friends, plus lots of fun at Toastmasters. On October 7, 1998, I "celebrated" my fifty-sixth birthday. To say that it wasn't a big deal would be a gross understatement. There was absolutely nothing celebratory.

Then came mail call, by which time I had become depressed and forlornly steeped in what my daughters call a pity party. I was called on the intercom to report to the officer's station to pick up my mail early. I couldn't believe what I saw: eighty-eight cards and letters. I read these with tears in my eyes, ashamed that I had felt so lonely and neglected. I realized that I am blessed with countless faithful and concerned friends who have struggled as much as they can through this ordeal with me, each step of the way.

The day after my birthday, there was another avalanche of mail. In all, somewhere between 150 and 200 birthday greetings were received. I have many blessings to count.

## Appeal News

I am told that the government has filed a slipshod reply to the brief filed on my behalf. My reply is due Friday, October 16. As it is filed, we will ask for assignment for oral argument as soon as possible. A final decision at or shortly after the year's end still looks possible, unless the government seeks more delays.

The hearing on oral argument will be in New Orleans at the Fifth Circuit Court of Appeals on Lafayette Square, just across from my office. It will be open to the public and will last a couple hours. Banner waving and cheers are frowned upon, but prayers would be appreciated.

## Insight

A counterpoint to the cynicism that runs wild here comes from the recent Insight program. Suffice it to say that I saw the lives of twenty men transformed in three days. It was an exhausting experience but well worth the effort.

The participant for whom I was the assigned "angel" was a black guy about forty years old. His story of suffering and unfair treatment was truly heartbreaking. He found great support from unlikely sources—mostly white guys who sympathized with him and offered encouragement. He blossomed and will no doubt cope better with his incarceration as a result of his experience.

A new roommate appeared out of the blue. "Pierre" claims to have operated several restaurants in New Orleans. He has taken a great interest in my case and anyone in Louisiana politics that I know. He asks way too many questions. I am staying as far away from him as I can. I don't mean to be unkind, but he has all the signs of a professional snitch.

October 1998

## Hurricane Georges

Although we had thirty-two inches of rain, we had little wind and no real damage. The greatest danger came from inmate tension, from being boarded up in the dorms for several days while Georges decided where to go. With the power off, we waited in the dark. Fights resulting from frazzled nerves were common, especially around the one TV operating on auxiliary power.

Finally, on the Wednesday after the storm passed, we were sent back to work. With all the rain, I looked forward to days of road repairs on the base and on our half-mile track. The first priority was to repair the dirt road to the trash dump so that hurricane debris could be removed.

The official estimate of the necessary repair time was one week. I told the chief that I could have it repaired in two hours. He laughed and told me to go for it. Over the next two and a half days, by starting early and going late, I repaired that road plus every other road on the base.

When I checked the equipment in with the chief, he was all worked up. The base commander had inspected the roads before the repairs and had applied for a large disaster relief allocation that was to be documented with photographs. Unfortunately, the disaster relief photographers arrived to take their pictures just after I had finished all the repairs.

The disaster funds were canceled. The chief got raked over the coals for repairing the roads too quickly and much too cheaply. He ordered me to not repair anything in the future without permission.

## Theology and Sanity

One of my salvaged religious books is *Theology and Sanity* by Frank Sheed. While slowly reading this interesting book, I have also been reading a little book on the theology of waiting. They both make the point, new to me, that much of our temporal and spiritual lives are spent *waiting*.

I am coming to understand the importance of "purposeful waiting." The trick is to find real meaning in the long periods that come between the flashes of brilliant insight and spectacular accomplishment. As I drift through a seemingly endless period of waiting, the challenge is to find meaning and to embrace each day until it is over.

> Habakkuk promises that the wait will not be in vain:
> How long, O Lord, must I cry for help
> > and you do not listen?
> Or cry out to you, "Violence!"
> > and you do not intervene?
> Why do you let me see iniquity?
> > why do you simply gaze at evil?
> Destruction and violence are before me;
> > there is strife and discord . . .
> Then the Lord answered and said:
> > Write down the vision;
> Make it plain upon tablets,
> > so that the one who reads it may run.
> For the vision is a witness for the appointed time,
> > a testimony to the end; it will not disappoint.

OCTOBER 1998

> If it delays, wait for it,
>> it will surely come, it will not be late.
> See, the rash have no integrity;
>> but the just one who is righteous because of his
>>> faith, shall live.  (1:2-3; 2:2-4)

## Hitchhiking

Just after the hurricane, while working on the roads, I got sunk in mud all the way up to the floor of the cab of the grader. I was at the bottom of a steep hill outside the gate, wedged against a tree and about three feet deep in the mud. It would be a long, hot walk back to the base.

Almost as soon as I began walking, a car came along bearing the Navy MWR (Morale, Welfare, and Recreation) logo. Two men stopped and offered me a ride. Ordinarily we are forbidden to talk with any non-BOP personnel. I decided that, to save a lot of time, hitching a ride was okay.

As we began to drive, I was extremely uncomfortable and uncharacteristically quiet. The two men in the car obviously recognized me as one the of the prisoners and were full of questions. I realized that, for almost ten months, I have had no conversations except with prison officials, inmates, and official visitors. Chatting with strangers felt uncomfortable and awkward.

This is, I assume, one of the symptoms of being institutionalized. I suspect that the longer I remain in this unusual setting, the longer it will take to return to normal. I am more ready than ever to give reacclimating a try.

# 17

# November 1998

It seems impossible that I have been here in paradise for almost a year. At the same time, I can hardly remember what it was like to lead a normal life. I am still doing well in almost every way, although I find myself missing some advantages of independent living, like an occasional scotch on the rocks.

## The Prison Reform Legislation

A rumor ran wild here during October that sixteen thousand nonviolent first offenders would receive pardons in order to make room in crowded prisons for real criminals. The rumor was based on a proposal made several years ago that died in committee. But hope clings to the most tenuous and insubstantial thread.

I tried to be gentle in discouraging this talk, but the rumors grew. Notices appeared on bulletin boards with details. Departing prisoners claimed to be leaving pursuant to the new legislation. A near frenzy developed.

November 1998

When the supposed release date of November 3 came and went, some guys looked as if they would go over the edge. There was a cruelty to this hoax that was distressing and pitiful. Hope is necessary, but deliberately fostering false hope is demonic.

## The Mighty Oak

One of my roommates presented me with an oak "tree": it is about two inches high and has only two clover-sized leaves. He grew it from an acorn. I was moved by his kindness and consideration, but he ruined it all when he announced that I would still be here when the tree was big enough for me to sit in its shade to read.

After riotous laughter, another roomie speculated that a better use for the tree would be to make an oak coffin out of it, since the need would coincide with my release. These guys are really a riot.

## Scriptural Inspiration

After reading the plaintive cry in Habakkuk that I shared last month ("How long, O Lord ..."), I decided to write a Faithwalk column about the theology of waiting. Waiting, waiting, waiting. It never seems to end, and it can be a time of despair, depression, and loss of hope.

The great challenge of faith is to wait patiently and purposefully. Sometimes I succeed, and at others I seem to fail miserably. At least by being here I have identified the challenge and given it a name: waiting. Since waiting is such a common curse, it is worth thinking about.

## The Big Question

In early November I had a nice visit from my daughter Beth and her boyfriend, André, aka Rocky. They both seemed a little giddy and nervous as we chatted. Finally Rocky took out a cigar and offered it to me, mumbling something about it being appropriate for the occasion. He explained that he had known Beth a long time and felt that they were meant for each other. After the awkwardness passed, we (even Beth) celebrated with cigars.

At one point, Rocky sat alone in the visiting yard, and I had the "Hispanic Mafia"—a group of six husky, tattooed weightlifters—surround him and question him about his intentions. They commented in Spanish on whatever he said.

Rocky used his fluent Spanish to turn the tide against me and to make new friends. He did seem, however, to have an excessive amount of perspiration on his brow when Beth and I rescued him.

## Thanksgiving Feast

The featured smoked turkey wings and legs were wonderful. The inmates cooked them in homemade smokers, and they were somehow kept moist and juicy. We also had corn, peas, salads, turkey soup (made with real stock), sweet and mashed potatoes, fresh rolls with gravy, and bakery-fresh pies topped with ice cream. There were also barrels of mixed nuts in the shell and peppermint candy.

It was a real feast, with indigestion for all! I don't know how much our regular $2.50 food budget was stretched, but it was great.

# 18

# December 1998

Merry Christmas and Happy New Year from paradise! In a lavish program jointly sponsored by the BOP and Navy HMW (Health, Morale and Welfare), the Christmas decorations featured a six-inch-square plastic Santa decal and a small Christmas tree decal stuck on the front door of Dorm C. The comedians in the dorm love to move the decals around to all kinds of clever places.

We will have lots of religious services during the season. This includes a family country-and-western singing group, a bell choir, and about fifteen choirs from fundamentalist churches. For Catholics, the local bishop will come for the first time to celebrate Mass on Christmas Day, and our chaplain is on high alert for the event.

Christmas is difficult for most here, just as Thanksgiving was. The big problem is being idle as the government goes on thirty or forty days of "liberal leave." This means that the staff can stay home for any flimsy excuse. Many work details are shut down, and most men here would prefer to work than to be idle. Loneliness festers, tempers flare, and depression is epidemic. Grasping attempts at holiday cheer magnify all that we have lost.

If it isn't too late, please don't send me a Christmas card. I normally get lots of mail, but the hacks hate the extra work. As Christmas tension builds, the recipient of excess cards can count on extra strip searches, garbage details, locker shakedowns, drug and alcohol tests, and midnight flashlight-in-the-face identity confirmations. I know well the fervent prayers and kindness you have showered on my girls and me during this difficult year. Nothing more is needed.

## Zoo News

This week two of my roomies went home. This is always bittersweet for those left behind. Andrew will go back to his work as a golf course designer and golf pro. He is extremely bitter about his case and what he sees as continuing harassment by the IRS.

Bubba will go back to working as a roofer in rural south Florida. He was an ardent hunter and outdoorsman, but now he will simply watch and enjoy nature. While here, he read everything on nature that he could find. He had access to the creek north of the camp and often smuggled bread out of the mess hall to feed the critters and fish.

I experienced a surprising sense of loss when these guys left. I hope they have enough of their former lives left intact so as to rebuild quickly. The good news is that the departures made a bottom bunk available, and my roomies agreed that I should have first crack at it. I now have the luxury of a place to sit and a night light, so that I can read at night.

In addition, I won't be freezing at night, as the AC vent no longer blows directly on me. I also now have my locker right next to the bed, which is convenient.

December 1998

In a lifestyle with few amenities or pleasures, the small things become intensely satisfying. This amazes me. The more we have, the less satisfying it becomes; and the less we have, the more we achieve peace by intensely appreciating and enjoying what we often took for granted, starting with the gift of life itself.

I decided to write about being thankful for my next column in the *Kenner Star*. This came after realizing how much I enjoy my two watts of light at night, having a place to sit on the bed, and other small joys.

## Turf Wars

Gregorio, a delightful, urbane, and well-educated Greek who has become a naturalized citizen, is one of the new safety office workers. I really enjoy his gentleness and humor. Since I was a veteran when he arrived, I have tried to befriend him.

Gregorio took over the recycling operation last week, attacking it with enthusiasm. As an ardent environmentalist, he thinks of his garbage sorting as a "refuse audit" that will benefit future generations. The operation now runs smoothly, and collections of recyclables have doubled.

Gregorio is organized and has free time, so he decided to beautify the recycling center by making flower beds at the entrance, where litter used to accumulate. With commendable effort and resourcefulness, he scrounged plants and bushes to make two large flower beds. The warden came by on one of her unannounced inspections and praised him lavishly and appropriately.

All was well in paradise until the foreman in charge of landscaping on the base happened by and went ballistic. He said the beautiful garden was "unauthorized" because his permission had not been obtained before construction began.

Gregorio endured the tongue-lashing calmly and then began digging up his creation, as ordered. In the "God Never Sleeps" category, the warden brought a visitor to see the product of Gregorio's ingenuity as it was being destroyed. She countermanded the hack's order, the garden was saved, good has triumphed over evil, and virtue has been rewarded. Hooray!

## Merry Christmas and Happy New Year!

On behalf of all the Cleveland Clan, I want to wish you all a Merry and Peaceful Christmas and a Happy New Year. My family and I appreciate the remarkable kindness shown by so many during our period of struggle, sadness, and turmoil. I hope that time is coming to an end.

With the help of the prayers and good wishes of faithful friends and family, we will not only survive but also grow and benefit from the experience we have shared. I look forward to the future with eager anticipation and buoyant hope, confident that my lonely journey has a meaning and purpose that will one day be clear. Thanks to all!

# 19

# January 1999

Who would have thought that in one year I could learn to type, lose fifty pounds, get in physical shape, write about twelve hundred letters, find spiritual peace, start a newspaper column, and be designated the official Navy road grader?

There are, of course, some significant negatives, but I try not to dwell on them. Suffice it to say that I have cried more in the last twelve months than in the rest of my life combined. But even in profound sadness, I have discovered the limitless kindness of many and the truth that I am not alone. I have saved every letter and card I have received and will always treasure them.

Essential lessons in life become easier to learn from a position of poverty of spirit, which comes with the turf here. This concept from the Beatitudes in Matthew 5 was something I had a hard time grasping before prison. Now I understand. It is only after experiencing utter powerlessness that we truly experience the goodness of God. Sometimes I feel hypocritical in wanting so earnestly to leave here, but then I recall that Jesus left the desert after forty days and nights.

On Christmas Day the local bishop came to celebrate Mass for us. This was his first visit, so everyone was excited and filled with eager anticipation. The "Moron Tabernacle Choir"—our terrible but loud and enthusiastic ensemble—was to sing. At the last minute, Kitty and Mel volunteered to drive to Pensacola early Christmas morning to provide music for us. It was truly a blessed moment. Bishop Ricard from Baton Rouge was great, and for her effort, Kitty was elevated to the rank of Most Favorite Daughter.

"Conflicts letters" have gone out for the argument of my appeal during the first week of March. This is ninety days behind schedule, but it's here at last. The oral argument is usually limited to twenty minutes per side. We have four parties to share the time, so a request for additional time will be made soon. Optimism runs high, but the tension is mounting.

# 20

# February 1999

The oak tree that a roommate gave me is thriving. It is now dark green, three inches high, and sporting four leaves. Each day I put it on the windowsill for sunshine; at night I put it on my locker.

Unfortunately, one day out of the blue, a diligent hack remembered the BOP rule against having vegetable matter in the dorms. The oak was summarily seized and written up. I eventually charmed the corrections officer into believing that the oak tree was harmless and could be released to the greenhouse, where it will have friends and will be watered automatically. But I have to admit that I have been a little lonesome since my small green friend was moved out of my room.

## March 3 Scripture Readings

I have developed the habit of reading the Scripture readings assigned for Mass each day in Catholic churches all over the world. When an important date is established, I read ahead for prophetic passages. March 3 is the day it will be decided whether or not I will be resurrected from oblivion to a normal life. The readings are interesting—in fact, *astounding!*

In the first reading, Jeremiah 18:18-20, Jeremiah laments that those he has treated justly are plotting to discredit him with his own innocent words. It's not a large stretch to recognize the use by the government of my recorded words of complex—but perfectly legal—tax advice to convict me. Jeremiah asks, "Must good be repaid with evil, that they should dig a pit to take my life?" (18:20).

The next reading for March 3 is Psalm 31. The psalmist declares that he will be freed "from the net they have set for me" (31:5). He then makes the ultimate faith commitment: he surrenders his own will and, as a precursor to the last words of Jesus Christ, says, "Into your hands I commend my spirit" (31:6).

He continues, "I hear the whispers of the crowd; terrors are all around me. They conspire together against me; they plot to take my life" (31:14). This is probably an apt description of my feelings and of the strategic planning of the prosecutors. The reading ends with Jeremiah observing, "I say, 'You are my God.' My destiny is in your hands; rescue me from my enemies, from the hands of my pursuers" (31:15-16).

When I first read this passage, it gave me pause. Many times over the last three-and-a-half years I have prayed, "Into your hands I commend my spirit." This is my last conscious thought each night. I have struggled mightily to surrender to whatever my fate might be. This is difficult when our lives don't go as we planned. Could it be mere coincidence that these readings will be read at Mass worldwide on March 3?

The real challenge comes from the Gospel reading for the day. It is Matthew 20:17-28. Jesus predicts his unjust condemnation and death by crucifixion after torture and public humiliation. Then he issues the ultimate challenge, which must have made his faithful disciples' blood run cold: "Can you drink of the cup that I am to drink?" (20:22).

I must admit that this passage frightened me. How will I hold up if my torture is not at an end but is only beginning? Although I hope with great expectation that my imprisonment is close to its end, I am braced to dig deep into personal resources that I'm not sure I possess. I strive to hang in there, no matter what comes. This is, after all, the great challenge of our faith.

## The Great HVAC Victory

Our antiquated HVAC system, a holdover from World War II, simply recirculates the stale air in the rooms. To get fresh air, we have to leave the two windows in the room open day and night (unless there is a hard rain) and block the door open.

During the unseasonably warm weather in January, the open doors provided some relief. Then the hacks, citing nonexistent "safety rules," started requiring that all doors be kept closed at all times. We were threatened with thirty hours of extra duty for everyone in the room if the door was cracked open. We were told with profanity that "inmates aren't entitled to fresh air."

Achievement Man to the rescue! Since I have a copy of the HVAC regulations, I carefully read them and discovered that there was an absolute requirement that each room benefit from eighty cubic feet per minute of outside air. I have a safety office measuring device that quantifies air flow electronically. With both windows fully open, we only get about 10 percent of the required circulation.

It seems that there was an old regulation that the doors have automatic closers when the buildings are without sprinklers.

Since the dorms have had sprinklers for eight years, no doors were required at all.

I typed a full-page memo for the safety director, outlining the whole problem. The hacks struck back by removing all doors they had previously kept closed. But since the doors are a safety device to prevent the spread of smoke during a fire, the inmates won again. When the hacks retaliated by ignoring the open-door policy, I posted a copy of the safety office memo on all dormitory bulletin boards. Victory is now complete and very sweet.

I got my report card covering the last six months and was encouraged by my "progress." My "institutional adjustment" has been good, and my custody level is "Min/Out," whatever that means. I do apparently have a blemish on my record for not enrolling in the drug abuse program. Not having ever used drugs is not considered an excuse, especially since this makes me easier to cure. Cures are statistically good.

My release preparation program will start in 2004. I will learn skills like opening a checking account and buying car insurance. One of my team's targeted goals for me is to join Toastmasters in the next six months. The fact that I'm in Toastmasters and have been elected vice president is no excuse.

It is officially noted that I have made progress since my last report by writing the A&O Manual, among other things. My teacher's personal note says, "Keep up the good work." My mother is proud.

## The Great Glue Caper

One of my greatest perks is being custodian of the safety office Krazy Glue. This stuff is priceless when it comes to making all kinds of repairs. A third of a bottle of glue has lasted for almost a year.

Recently an inmate came to me to request some of the precious glue. The repairs are usually done in my presence, but I trusted this guy and let him take the glue away. He was gone for a week. When the glue turned up, it was half-empty and the spout broken. I was fuming.

A month went by, and the same guy again asked to use the glue. I started to say no but then decided to give him the benefit of the doubt. He promised to return it in ten minutes. When the glue reappeared a week later, this time it was completely empty.

The guy said the glue must have spilled without his noticing. I was furious, and I told every inmate who came to me for glue that he had stolen the whole supply and was selling it. They were all just as angry, and I felt justified.

Then one day Paul, my career criminal/philosopher friend, gently told me to let go of my anger or I would suffer for it. He also suggested that I get another bottle of glue. His suggestion seemed impossible.

I went to my boss, the safety director, and told him sheepishly that I was out of glue. His response was to immediately give me a new bottle. I was stunned. My anger had been making me miserable. The issue was no big deal until I let it become one.

Paul was right. There is so much Christian wisdom on this topic. Live and learn, even here.

# 21

# March 1999

The Really Big News is that Trish Cleveland, daughter number four and a nurse in California, has accepted a marriage proposal from her long-time boyfriend, Todd. I met Todd a few months before coming here, and he has visited me here. He has handled my circumstances well.

I recently got a message to call Todd, and I suspected why. After a painful pause on the phone, he professed his undying love, respect, admiration, and cosmic bond with Trish in positively poetic terms. I am thrilled for them and dream regularly about lots of grandchildren, which will spectacularly increase our redfish limit for post-prison fishing adventures.

### Appeal News

Time hung heavy as I awaited the March 3 oral argument in the Fifth Circuit Court of Appeals. It went well, but nothing definitive happened. Many thanks to the faithful mob who showed up for the hearing to shout, "Free Willie!"

Questions were relatively few, perhaps because of heavy media coverage. Optimism is high, but I must wait two to four months for a decision. I am peaceful and calm, having morphed from the world's most impatient person into a casual "waiter."

The playful harassment from my roommates is unending. They are pulling for me with great enthusiasm. All predict my release soon, and most want help with their own legal machinations after I go home.

My great challenge is to be equally well-prepared for victory or defeat. This is without doubt the most difficult challenge that I have ever encountered.

Other than the appeal tension, life here is basically unchanged, and the search for meaning continues. My mind tells me daily that I have been planted here for a reason and have not been abandoned or forgotten by God, but my faith falters at times.

The "Super Snitch," an inmate whom some of you visitors have grown to know and love, was miraculously released last week. It seems that this prince went back to court to testify against his brother. The brother got a thirty-year sentence, and my "friend" got a year off his sentence. He was sent to a halfway house.

## Help from Yamashita

Reading a new fictional but historically accurate biography of General MacArthur helps put my struggles in perspective. My burdens and pains fade into wisps of smoke in comparison to the suffering on both sides during and after the war in the Pacific. That conflict produced unimaginable suffering for military personnel and civilians alike.

I am impressed by General Yamashita, the famous Tiger of Malaysia, who captured Singapore from the British defenders even though he was outnumbered three to one. Then he joined the battle in the Philippines, where he held out until after the Japanese surrendered. He was a brilliant and brave leader, and he did all in his power to prevent further atrocities as the tide of the war turned against the Japanese.

Nevertheless, because of MacArthur's vanity and hatred, Yamashita was tried as a war criminal. Facts were ignored, and MacArthur saw to it that he would be hanged. The Japanese joined in to persecute him, but through it all Yamashita maintained his dignity, calmly asserted his innocence, and accepted his fate. History has judged him kindly, and he is honored in death.

Somehow the extreme suffering and obvious injustice endured by so many throughout history make my predicament more bearable.

## Kitty's Stage Triumph

Kitty has been in numerous stage productions over the years. Last month she had her biggest and best role as Golde, the female lead in *Fiddler on the Roof*, at the Jefferson Performing Arts Society. All who attended raved about her acting and singing. I did miss being there, but I hope there will be other plays.

We who are lucky enough to be closely associated with Kitty know what a reach it was for her to "play" a pushy Jewish mother type. I am immensely proud of her and her drive to teach at SLU, sing professionally, and be a homemaker and stepmother.

MARCH 1999

## BOP Dental Care

Last month I got really sick for the first time due to an abscess in my right lower molars. After hours of waiting, I was finally seen by a dental assistant, who told me the dentist would not be in for several days. She could see that I was in pain, with considerable swelling in my cheek and neck. An x-ray confirmed the problem, so she called the dentist for suggestions. I felt ashamed that I had so often ridiculed health services here.

I was told the dentist would prescribe antibiotics and pain medication, but I would have to wait over the weekend, till he came in on Tuesday. A helpful inmate suggested leaving aspirin tablets on the sore spot to dissolve. This gave great but temporary relief.

When I went for my appointment, I was told after a long wait that there had been a mix-up; the dentist was not in. I got another appointment for a couple days later. By then I had treated myself with salt water, and the severe aspirin burns to my gums had apparently done some good with the infection. Then there unfolded events that could only happen here.

I arrived for my dental care at about 1:30 p.m. The dentist called for my chart and saw that the two assistants, after my x-rays and a previous consultation with him, had noted a probable abscess. He was incensed that they had "diagnosed" my ailment.

For two hours the dentist chewed out his assistants and made them read multiple policy manuals. They were in tears, saying that they had told me that an official diagnosis would be made by the dentist. Then the dentist, who had not seen a single patient the entire afternoon, announced that it was three o'clock, and he was leaving.

As the dentist walked out, he told me to open my mouth. He looked in and asked how I was doing. I replied that the pain had subsided somewhat after about ten days with the aspirin. To my amazement, he then declared that I was no longer an emergency and would have to make a written request for a regular appointment.

When I reacted with shock, he proudly informed me that during his tenure, the wait had been reduced from two years to only six months. During all my hours of waiting at his office, not a single inmate received treatment.

## Musings on the Future

What happens as a result of the hearing on March 3 will to a large extent shape the rest of my life. A reversal could mean exoneration and vindication. It could mean the culture shock of returning from the dead to a world that has survived fine without me.

I feel great anxiety as the fateful decision day approaches. I have absolutely no control over what will happen. I am in the position of a sick person undergoing life-threatening surgery. I simply submit and hope for the best.

Will I be fully restored? Will I die, in effect, or will I "awake" to some fate that I never even considered? The uncertainty and the stakes are less than pleasant. I want to get it over with.

# 22

# April 1999

I have to admit that time has dragged recently and tension has intensified as I await the decision of the Fifth Circuit Court of Appeals. There has been no news from the court except that the appeal was not summarily and immediately rejected. All I do now is wait, although my heart races each time I am paged over the intercom. In all likelihood, the decision is still thirty to sixty days away.

To pass the time, I stay as busy as possible and do structured workouts seven days a week. Time still drags, and I struggle to avoid even thinking about how wonderful it would be to go home.

The recent readings for Mass, especially during Holy Week, have been inspirational and moving. At times it is as though they are directed specifically at me and my situation, as well as my state of mind, which has swung wildly lately. Injustice and suffering are not unique to me.

Scriptural consolation is remarkably elastic and adaptable. I think I am beginning to get the point. We will always be disappointed if we rely on personal power or other sources of worldly security for our consolation. But we are never left unsatisfied if we rely on the mercy of our loving God to carefully guide us through life's challenges and then to gather each of us gently in his embrace. After we relax and surrender, we eventually achieve peace, a sense of purpose, the understanding that our suffering is a catalyst that forges spiritual maturity, and the true security of knowing that all will end well.

Kitty wrote a beautiful song for me, to help put perspective on my confinement. I won't let her sing it because I know it will make me cry. It is called "Surrender," and the lyrics are as follows:

> I had it all: fortune, power, acclaim,
> Worldly success, a respectable name.
> But then they vanished, illusions of safety.
> My spirit was crushed, nothing worldly could save me.
> How could this happen? They've taken my life.
> No justice found, hope barely alive.
> My heart was broken, my spirit despairing.
> I cried out, "My God, why have you forsaken me?"
> No answer came as the flames purified,
> Burning to ashes my false sense of pride.
> I never thought I really needed a Messiah.
> Now I saw clearly, illuminating fire.
> *Refrain:* Then came the peace, touched so deeply by your mercy.
> I lost my pride and found you're all I need.
> You rescued me, felt your love in my surrender.
> I reached my greatest height down on my knees.

## APRIL 1999

And so I gave you my life, my very soul,
Learning to let go, surrender control.
Then I took courage, though scorned and rejected,
For it's in my weakness that your power is perfected.
*Refrain:* Then came the peace, touched so deeply by your mercy.
I lost my pride and found you're all I need.
You rescued me, felt your love in my surrender.
I reached my greatest height down on my knees.[1]

---

1  For a free download of Kitty's song "Surrender," please go to www.kittycleveland.com/downloads.

# 23

# MAY 1999

After being here for this, my seventeenth month, I finally understand a mysterious reference in a John le Carré spy novel: the first week as a prisoner lasts a lifetime, but after that, time blurs and flies by without a conscious perception of its passage.

Time has flown in what seems an instant, yet I can hardly remember the old routines that once consumed my time, effort, and conscious thought. So now onto the random musings about the events of the month in my strange world.

## Joey's Pilgrimage

A highlight of Joey's trip to Rome was being present at the beatification of Padre Pio. The nun who was the subject of one of the official miracles attributed to his intervention was there in full habit. After a twenty-seven-foot fall from a ladder thirty years ago, she had been bedridden for three-and-a-half years, with serious blood clots in her injured leg. Following futile treatment, it was decided that her leg would have to be amputated.

The night before this surgery, a relic of Padre Pio was wrapped inside this nun's bandages while she and her friends prayed for divine intervention. The next morning, her terrible wounds had disappeared, and her clots had dissolved without a trace.

After medical confirmation, the nun became devoted to the cause of the sainthood of Padre Pio. She was given a glove worn by him during his lifetime to cover the marks of the stigmata on his palms, and she carried this relic on the trip to Rome. It emitted a powerful scent of roses.

For two weeks Joey and her friend Betty assailed the heavens with prayers at every major shrine of Christianity in Rome. They lit candles and sought the intercession of the good Padre in my cause. It will be interesting to learn what the answer to all these prayers will be.

## Saying "Thank You"

Fr. Joe, the chaplain here, asked me to be one of several inmates to give a short speech to the 150 or so volunteers who have worked in various prison ministries. As I thought about what I would say to all these nice people, I choked up with emotion, just thinking about the kindness of these strangers. Finally I decided to write out what I wanted to say.

"Until coming here, I had no idea that all prison inmates—regardless of age, race, education, occupation, health, guilt, or innocence—have been shattered by their experience in varying ways and to varying degrees. We are lonely, dispirited, depressed, isolated from all we love, and generally sad, even when our tough facade or swaggering step might indicate otherwise. Soon most of us begin to feel useless and subhuman.

"And then you angels of mercy appear, without motive other than charity and concern, to show simply by your presence that we are not, in fact, abandoned or forgotten by our world or our God. On behalf of all whom you have touched and encouraged by your presence, I say, 'Thank you, and thank God for you.'

"Before coming here, I was the one who ministered to others in need—in youth groups, schools, church, hospitals, work, and my family. Now I, too, understand what it means to have someone reach out when I am in need."

I became overwhelmed with emotion before I finished reading, but I think the people got the point. And I feel the same way about you who have been kind to me through it all. Heartfelt thanks to all of you. With the help of so many, how can I fail to survive?

## Good News

I found a place in the greenhouse where my little tree gets lots of sun and is undisturbed. It is growing rapidly, and it now has sixteen to eighteen leaves. It is beautiful. Somehow it has become a symbol of hope for me. If I am released, I will bring it home and transplant it in the yard as a lasting reminder of God's faithfulness.

Mother's Day here was a beautiful, clear, and cool day. Joey, Kitty, and Caitlin all visited. It had been a month since Caitlin could visit because of her busy practice and game schedule, and Joey had been on her trip to Rome for several weekends. I missed them.

The girls were full of news. They sang beautifully at the Mother's Day Mass. All the mothers received a potted geranium, grown by Grumpy.

# 24

# June 1999

Time seems to drag maddeningly as I await the appellate court decision. I have a recurring thought that if we win, I could have a heart attack from the months of tense waiting. I'll add more aerobic workouts this week. And I'll be sure to take deep breaths when the time comes.

One of the most interesting characters I have met here is "Peanut" from Louisiana, who got six months for catching too many fish at the mouth of the Mississippi. Now that the government has branded him a renowned fisherman, Peanut is going to get into the fishing guide business. I will send out his grand opening rate schedule to my fishing-fanatic friends.

## Emotion Control

As I have acclimated to being powerless, my whacked-out emotions have gradually recovered. Recently, however, I have felt tears well up unexpectedly as I think about the past and the future and the prospect of being here for most of a decade. Then I realized that part of the clever government effort to break our spirit and will is to show tearjerker movies at our weekly screenings.

When I talked with Joey about the highly emotional movies we were seeing, she didn't think they sounded so bad. I will watch *Old Yeller* this week with an open mind. But at this point I think that movie selection is done by the PsyOp guys from the BOP.

When a decision comes from the court of appeals, I expect to be paged to go to the case manager's office. Each time the voice of a corrections officer blares an unintelligible demand over the intercom, my heart skips a beat. If I hear my name, I go into cardiac arrest and breathe deeply as I report to find out the news. This happens several times each week.

Last week, when I was ordered to "report to the unit secretary immediately!" I hurried in and was told that there was a document that required my signature. An official-looking government document facing me said, "ORDER FOR IMMEDIATE RELEASE." I grabbed a pen and started signing. But that document wasn't for me.

My emergency signing event was for a letter from my attorneys. It was only an "intercom emergency" because the secretary wanted to go home early.

## The New Roomie

After a delay of several weeks and much speculation, a new inmate was assigned to my dorm room, bringing us back up to our quota of eight residents. The poor guy was in a complete daze after spending eight months in the Escambia County Jail while his case was resolved. He is a professorial-looking, thirty-five-year-old white guy with horn-rimmed glasses, a ready smile, and a wife who is

## June 1999

terminally pregnant. His offense involved smuggling drugs from California to Florida.

Our new roomie won everyone's heart by asking that we pray for the guys who had become his friends in the county jail. They would never have the good fortune to become federal prisoners in a camp setting with at least minimal freedom and the chance to be busy each day with work and classes.

# 25

# July 1999

I hoped to be home by now—fishing, cooking on the grill, watching Caitlin's basketball games, and avoiding wedding preparations. I'm still here, and another round of brief writing may cause further delays. But a new US Supreme Court decision by a rare unanimous court is favorable to my position and directly relevant to my appeal.

My attorneys have filed a supplemental brief (one of about six since oral argument), and the government will doubtless demand weeks to respond. For now I can relax, get back into my usual routine, and forget about news, good or bad.

### Pierre's Disturbing Death

On June 14, at about 8 a.m., my roommate Pierre, the restaurateur from New Orleans, began to have severe stomach and chest pains. He was having what is now described as an abdominal aneurysm. The BOP medical assistants, who spend their time mainly classifying inmate illnesses as malingering or non-emergencies, failed to render any assistance. They declared the problem a kidney stone, for which Pierre had no history, and overlooked a heart problem, for which Pierre had a long history—including three prior heart attacks for which he was taking medication. He was not examined, medicated, or tested in any way.

As his pain became unbearable, Pierre tried several times to get medical assistance. Each try failed. By 2 p.m. he was writhing on the floor in agony, unable to speak or even climb into his bunk.

A couple other guys and I carried Pierre to the medical department and demanded that the staff do something. We repeatedly said that he was having chest pains and had a history of heart attacks. The response was still a casual indifference and reluctance to become involved.

An hour later, Pierre was finally driven to the hospital by one of the hacks. There he bled to death, still without any medical care. No one examined him despite six hours of agony and desperate pleas for help.

Pierre was only fifty-six years old. His family will probably never know what happened to him. At his memorial service, with the staff present, one inmate accused the BOP of murdering Pierre with a lethal combination of ineptitude and indifference. It caused quite a stir, but so far there has been no retaliation against him for speaking the truth. He is just finishing his sentence and will most likely go home soon.

## Lucky the Laugher

Our new roomie, Lucky, has a brightly enthusiastic, positive attitude. He has apparently never had a job other than in the drug trade. He is about forty-seven and eagerly looks forward to his release in a few years so that he can get a real job.

Lucky's first prison job, in typical BOP fashion, is as a mechanic. He admits to knowing absolutely nothing about engines. But after two days on the job, he has gotten his pregnant wife to make a deposit on a garage in his hometown, in anticipation of buying and operating the business when he is released. This quick step was based on his ecstasy after changing three flat tires and putting new spark plugs in a riding lawnmower.

Last night Lucky asked for help in selecting a name for his soon-to-be-born daughter. His present wife, number five, feels that since he is the lord and master of the marriage, he should make all important decisions. So Lucky decided to name his daughter Sonya, in honor of the female DEA agent who busted him and sent him to jail. This seemed a little strange to me but perfectly logical to Lucky.

The unusual experiences that are commonplace in my room will supply me with more than enough material for a TV prison sitcom. Of course, no one would believe that the characters are real!

# 26

# Kitty: Grace for Whatever Comes

We all waited anxiously for the Fifth Circuit Court of Appeals to reverse my dad's convictions and send him home to us. When I stopped in to visit my mom, she was standing at the kitchen counter, and she looked at me with a desperation that startled me.

"If we lose the appeal, Kitty, I'm not going to make it," she confessed. "I can't keep living like this!"

She put her head on my shoulder, and we both began to cry. The uncertain future; the financial instability; the long drives back and forth to Pensacola; the endless waiting; and the toll it had taken on the mental, emotional, and physical health of each member of the family—Mom just couldn't do it anymore. The thought of another seven or eight years of this anguish was too much to bear.

And then came a special gift, an insight that did not come from me.

"Mom, we don't have the grace for that yet."

We pulled apart from our embrace and looked each other in the eye.

"We can't project ourselves into the future, imagining every horrible thing, before we have the grace for it. If we do, we'll be paralyzed with fear and anxiety—and it's not even real!"

Mom nodded.

"Well, all right then," I continued. "We just have to trust that God will give us the grace for whatever comes, when we need it. He's going to take care of us, just as he has every day till now. 'Give us *this day our daily* bread,' we pray, and he will continue to provide for us one day at a time."

A couple weeks later, we got the call we were dreading.

# 27

# July 22, 1999

Today I got the devastating news that my appeal was *denied*. For once in my life, I am at a loss for words to explain what has happened to me, how I feel about it, or how I will cope with the future. I have confidence that through faith, strength will come to me and to my wonderful family and friends.

I do believe that my heart stopped beating when I first heard the news. It was difficult to breathe and impossible to think. With a little time to adjust, I have resolved to hold on and to continue to stay busy and positive. I hear that the court's decision was one-sided and shallow, and I don't intend to read it anytime soon. Of the dozens of serious issues raised, none was won.

It will take some adjustment to hunker down for the long term, but for now, there is no other realistic option. This setback will be hardest on Joey and the girls. I ask that you keep them in your prayers and provide them with support in any way you reasonably can. We will all adjust and strive to avoid losing hope. No easy task but doable.

My dark night of the soul continues. As I sit here thinking about the future, an otherworldly sense of peace surrounds me. I know that I am not alone. My fervent prayer is for the strength to provide a positive example of cheerful endurance for the long haul. I will focus on my release date of October 8, 2006, one day after my sixty-fourth birthday, and will conquer one day at a time.

## My Faithwalk Article for September, "Dealing with Disaster: Romans 8:28"

On July 22, my family and I experienced one of those gut-wrenching catastrophes that befall many of us at one time or another. It blots out the sun, and we feel despair, shock, fear, and anger—as if we have been kicked in the stomach. We ponder how a loving God could permit this to happen to us.

When it happened to me, I couldn't breathe. I thought my heart would stop beating. I am separated from my wife and family by hundreds of miles and feel hopelessly alone.

As I struggled numbly for equilibrium, I turned to my Scripture reading for the day. Later on I found out that my wife had done the same exact thing at almost the same exact time. By coincidence, we both picked Romans 8:28. This is a favorite passage for those in crisis and is familiar to most people of faith.

This simple passage can seem senseless at times and is difficult to embrace enthusiastically, even for those with repeated experiences of the wonderful truth of its proclamation, "We know that all things work for good for those who love God, who are called according to his purpose." How much simpler and peaceful life would be for us if we could totally accept this promise and incorporate it into our everyday lives once and for all.

## July 22, 1999

St. Paul looks at the central problem of prayer. How are we to know what to pray for? Television, novels, magazines, and popular culture all answer this question very easily. We will be happy if we have great wealth, beauty, success, power, fame, and possessions.

We all know that this is not necessarily so. The object of our heart's desire can turn out to be a catastrophe when we get what we pray for. It may be the worst spouse, job, or satisfied wish we could imagine.

Pop culture will never accept the proposition that good can come from apparent evil or that happiness grows out of no-holds-barred catastrophe or failure. How can modern people of faith make sense out of this passage? The answer for me came in a flash of new insight as I suffered and struggled in a crisis that continues to this day.

St. Paul suggests that in evaluating life's problems and events, both good and bad, one focal question should always be asked first: Does this event unite me with God or separate me from him? Stated slightly differently, when we are devastated, we should repeat a fundamental faith proposition over and over to ourselves: "In the end, the only thing that matters is whether we achieve salvation in the time allotted to us for our lives."

Salvation is not dependent upon whether our friends and neighbors think we are successful, or whether we are rich and famous and beautiful and healthy. Rather it depends upon whether we use the events of our lives to conform our minds to the mind of God. Every experience can bring us closer to our loving Creator if our attitude is right.

There is a puzzling paradox here. Being overly successful in the ways of the world causes most of us the most trouble. It is our successes that make us forget our utter dependence upon our Creator.

Our gifts can focus us inward, on what we pridefully perceive as our own powers, quite easily separating us from God and his will for us.

The other side of this paradox is the good news. If we turn to God with expectant faith and trusting acceptance when unspeakable disaster strikes, we always find him there with a warm and reassuring embrace. Disaster is, in fact, the perfect medium for an encounter with God. We are open, maybe desperately so, and he is present and eager to lead us in a direction totally consistent with our whole purpose for living and dying—our personal salvation.

We can look back on past disasters and recognize that out of those conflagrations have often come great good that we could never have envisioned when the problem first overwhelmed us. As these experiences accumulate, faith becomes "easier."

Romans 8:28 is a great consolation for anyone in crisis. Hang in. Hang on. Trust God, and he will reveal where it is that he would like our lives to go. We needn't struggle against him or be angry with him. God knows in a way that we never will be able to comprehend how the events of our lives can bring us closer to our eventual union with him. Nothing counts except whether we are moving toward God or retreating from him. All events, both good and bad, are designed to have the same effect if we have faith. Easier said than done, but practice makes perfect.

We can follow the example of Jesus and pray as he did during his great passion and suffering, "Into your hands, O Lord, I commend my spirit. Your will, not mine, be done" (see Luke 23:46; 22:42).

# 28

# AUGUST 1999

This letter is more difficult to write than the first one I wrote, over eighteen months ago. My feelings are hard to describe. The system to which I devoted thirty-five years of my life has failed me. I have been unjustly convicted of a crime I did not commit. I am confronted with the daunting prospect of being imprisoned for ten years, with little possibility of a time reduction for "good behavior."

My first feeling was that this is grossly unfair and disgusting. I must admit to feeling sorry for myself and for my family, friends, and all who have supported me through everything. Think of all the sincere—but apparently unanswered—prayers!

Then a flood of simple and eloquent messages of support and compassion began to arrive. It was so overwhelming that for days I couldn't read most of them—and then only a few at a time, in private. As is expressed in the Faithwalk column for September, my thoughts turned to Romans 8:28 and its supreme consolation.

My health is still great. I will one day get to go home. I will be a much different person from the one who showed up here at Christmas in 1997. Never again will I take for granted my abundant blessings.

All is uncertain, but amazingly, I feel a pervasive sense of peace and some expectant anticipation. It will really be interesting to see what the future holds for me, after all that I was has been crushed into nothingness. It is entirely possible that the real purpose for my existence will be revealed as I apparently languish in lonely isolation. I am determined not only to survive but to do so with some sense of dignity and purpose. Perhaps my mission is nothing more than not giving up in despair and anger.

I don't feel that I deserve what has become my lot in life, but life is not fair. I could easily have been brought down by disease, personal disaster, a head-on crash with a drunk driver, or any number of random catastrophes that afflict many at one time or another. And what distinguishes my suffering from what most people suffer is the astounding level of continuing support I receive from my family and friends.

For months I prayed simply that God would let me go home. My new prayer is, "Into your hands, O Lord, I commend my spirit. Your will, not mine, be done." If I can truly incorporate this attitude into my life, something—and perhaps many great things—will happen.

My new station in life required some immediate action. I got new shoes, socks, and underwear at government expense. I have found consolation in outdoor physical labor, with the heat index hovering at 120 degrees on most days. I planted my first vegetable garden. Staying involved is necessary.

The Toastmasters Club reelected me as an officer (although my first reaction was to withdraw), and soon I will start the apprentice electrician's course that is taught by Electric Tommy, one of the real characters here.

## August 1999

My attorneys will work on a strategy for obtaining my release, and I will focus on sanity, faith, health, and constructive thought. When all is considered, the anguish of the moment will refocus and heighten the remainder of my life, much as appreciation of a cool glass of water can be heightened by a few days of crawling in the desert. Life's simple day-to-day pleasures, freedoms, joys, sorrows, relationships, and experiences are often lost in the confusion and busyness of daily routine. I will never have that problem again.

I can hardly contain myself when I think about how much joy I would find in drawing the duty of taking Caitlin to one of her seemingly endless practices or simply waking up in my own home again. I will doubtless lose at least 10 percent of my remaining life expectancy to unjust confinement, but the other 90 percent will be enhanced to the point that the loss will disappear in insignificance.

With the continued support of so many family members and friends to bear me up during the down days, failure is not an option. The future holds much that I cannot comprehend or even conceive of now. My sacred responsibility is to hang on and hang in resolutely and cheerfully, and I shall do so.

## Room Search

On a routine weeknight recently, one of the hacks came to our room to search all our lockers. Lucky had just bought several dollars' worth of freshly baked bread, jelly, and peanut butter from some scamming inmate. He had the misfortune to leave it in plain view in his locker. When the hack confronted him with this insidious contraband and demanded an explanation of what he was up to, Lucky came unglued. In one sentence he said, "I never saw it before.... I was going to eat it for breakfast.... It's not mine.... It belongs to Art."

Art had been out of the room but walked in at that moment. When asked if the contraband was his, Art said, "Yes," and proceeded to eat the entire loaf of bread and the whole jar of peanut butter, with some help from amused roommates. Lucky learned several important lessons in the art of survival.

## Off Base

A couple weeks ago, I had the emotional and unexpected fun of traveling off base to the aluminum recycler, to deliver fifteen hundred pounds of aluminum cans. It was an eerie experience to see the real world after so long an absence. Much has changed.

I understand, from inmates who got to take a five-day furlough during the last six months before release, that it is difficult to return home. They all feel as if the space they formerly occupied—as benevolent dictator/lord/king/boss/father/despot—has closed seamlessly in their absence, and they are in fact not only dispensable but sometimes hardly missed. This is a real blow and a difficult adjustment for most. All left behind grow wildly, while the returning inmate is frozen in the world that existed when he left. Lots of adjustment is required.

## Daughter News

Connie will soon start a new job as dorm mom and substitute teacher at St. Paul's School for boys. She will live on campus and care for eighth-grade Mexican boys who have come to the U.S. to learn English.

Caitlin recently played in a national AAU basketball tournament in Orlando. Her team qualified for the final championship series but was eliminated in two close games. Wait until next year, when Caitlin and her team return for their second year of competition in their age bracket!

Beth and Trish continue with wedding plans, with my brother Murray filling in for me at official functions.

Kitty got great reviews for her role as Mother Abbess in the Sound of Music at Tulane Summer Lyric. The newspaper review credited her with bringing the house down with a rousing rendition of "Climb Every Mountain."

Caroline is home for the summer and will go to Honduras with Connie for a week or so to work at a mission before returning to Vanderbilt for her junior year.

In closing, thanks again to all of you for your continuing support. Don't give in to discouragement!

## From Joey

I would like to add my appreciation to Carl's for the wonderful support we have received from so many caring and loving people. We could not continue in our daily walk without you and without our faith that somehow, in God's time, we will emerge from the fire unharmed, faith-filled, and ready to serve the Lord wherever he calls. We have grown spiritually in ways that would not have been possible if life had remained status quo.

Most of us don't volunteer to suffer, but when it is thrust upon us and we cannot escape, the Lord tests our hearts for faith, courage, strength, and commitment. And he will give us these attributes if we but ask him. The Lord is with us. We are NOT alone.

Our family has received much encouragement from all of you as well, and many difficult days have been lifted by a kind word received in a card or letter. We do need encouragement (literally, strengthening of our hearts) for this trial we have been given to endure. May God richly bless you all for the assistance you give to us, and may we one day be able to return the favor to you.

# 29

# SEPTEMBER 1999

I am typing on an early Sunday morning in mid-September, just after sunrise. The air today is cool and dry. The sky is clear, and the north wind is blowing. Just when it seemed that the humid, scorching summer would never end, relief is here.

All things in life end in due time, and it's reassuring to think that it is just as sure that my season of confinement and loneliness shall also end one day. In the meantime, there are countless blessings even here that I become more aware of as time passes. Amid maddening levels of bureaucratic ineptitude, this place brings the little joys of life into sharp focus.

First on my list is an overwhelming sense of gratitude for your faithful support. Your prayers, kind thoughts, and letters are a great source of inspiration and comfort. As I adjust my thoughts to being here for at least another year, and perhaps much longer, it helps to know that there are many who think my fate is unjust.

I am grimly determined to hang in and hang on without whining and complaining. Just as I feel my strength and energy returning a little each day with physical workouts, my spiritual and emotional strength grow a little each day as new challenges arise and are somehow met. I keep my focus on the short term and plow ahead.

As is usually the case, I thought there would be nothing left to talk about this month. But new adventures abound.

## Luxuries

Since I'm not going home soon, I reevaluated my personal possessions and decided to splurge on two wantonly hedonistic items that are available in the commissary here. I bought a small radio with headphones and a one-gallon, plastic, insulated jug. These are now sources of distraction and fun.

I fill the jug with apples, oranges, plums, peaches, and crushed ice. Now each night before lights out, I have an ice-cold fresh-fruit feast that is beyond description. I can trade other food or favors for various amounts of fresh fruit.

Then I discovered, through some trial and error, that I can use the insulated jug to cook, using much the same principles as the old, insulated Chambers ranges. I can get my intended food boiling hot and then put it in the jug to simmer for hours. Using purchases from the commissary, supplemented with vegetables and peppers from the greenhouse and my garden, plus occasional leftovers from the mess hall, truly creative prison cuisine is possible. My room has taken on the not-so-subtle aroma of minced garlic, peppers, onions, and tomatoes, rivaling the kitchen at Tony Angello's, my favorite Italian restaurant.

The radio is a little less successful. I got it to listen to Saints and Tulane football games, and both have done little but look hopeless and lose ever since. My effort to return the radio for a refund

September 1999

failed. Since then I have rediscovered the joy of classical music and interesting news commentary.

The radio also works in the Navy movie theater, where we have weekend movies from a video store. I never went to movies because of the noise level, which made it impossible to actually hear the movie dialogue. Now I get sound on my radio in stereo and shut out the background jungle noises. Life is good.

## More Heavy Equipment Licenses

Since the recycling detail that I helped organize deals in tons of cardboard, paper, pallets, scrap metal, and aluminum cans, we have frequent need for a forklift to move massive bales of material. The only practical solution was for someone of suitable age, experience, and discretion in the safety office to become a licensed forklift driver. Since I qualified, at least in the age category, I trained myself with a video and a training manual that I wrote last year.

There was something of a practical gap in my training, so I borrowed the keys to the beautiful forklift from the warehouse clerk and headed to a remote part of the base to practice maneuvers. Just as I gained shaky control of my mount, some Navy guys flagged me down and said they needed me to move some huge boxes stacked on pallets. Since I had not yet figured out the maze of controls for lifting, moving side-to-side, or tilting the forks, I was a little reluctant. They insisted, and I foolishly gave in instead of explaining my rookie status.

I got the forks under the boxes and found the lift control. Great fun! Then I discovered that the load totally obstructed my view to the front. The manufacturer must have anticipated this problem, and that's why the forklift will go so high.

I began lifting my load so that I could see under it, but it resisted. I gave it more gas, and it began to move. It was heavier than I would have guessed. Then I heard a strange "skroink" sound mixed with screams over the noise of the straining engine. My twelve-foot-high load had been lifted six additional feet under a sixteen-foot-high warehouse roof.

No real harm was done. They were able to re-nail the roof without too much difficulty.

Now I toss around two-thousand-pound loads like they're nothing. I have noticed that everyone stays well clear of my operations without having to be asked.

## The Victory Garden

My little garden passed its greatest challenge last week. A jealous inmate snitched to the dreaded SIS officer, Lieutenant Walker, that it existed. When the SIS chief noticed all the greenery and the unusual black dirt, he complimented us for our beautiful tomatoes and said his were not nearly as nice. Although private gardens are frowned upon, this one is outside the prison camp boundaries and was not a concern for him.

The garden lives and has a semi-official status now. It is growing wildly in all directions and amazes me with its daily changes. I hope tomatoes will soon be abundant.

For the past three weeks, on Thursday nights, I have cooked angel hair pasta with tomato and pepper sauce. It is now an obligation to make a wash tub of this stuff each week. In exchange, I get to participate in Nacho Night on Friday and Pizza Night on Sunday.

SEPTEMBER 1999

Cooking here is a challenge, since almost everything is illegal unless it comes from the commissary, and our only heat sources are hot water in the janitor's closet and microwave ovens in the dorms. My spaghetti sauce cooks for forty-eight hours in coffee pots, microwaves, and thermos jugs. The tomato sauce has fresh tomatoes, garlic, seasoned salt, Cajun spices, black pepper, fresh jalapeno, habanero, chili, cayenne and bell peppers from the garden, fresh and dried onions, green onions, celery from the salad bar, chicken stock from bouillon cubes, and Louisiana Hot Sauce.

After the sauce simmers for twenty-four hours, I add a combination of pepperoni, summer sausage, and canned chicken. A splash of sugar and some A1 steak sauce are the finishing touches. The pasta cooks fast, in a dishpan in a microwave.

Please don't try this in your home. The process is dangerous and requires the stomach of a turkey vulture and the hunger of a shipwreck victim. I knew my audience wasn't going to be finicky when no one cared that the coffee pot broke on the first batch and the broken glass that could be scooped from the surface was removed just before serving.

Every scrap gets eaten in nanoseconds. The spicier the better, as far as most are concerned. It's really too hot for me, but the eaters equate spiciness with manly goodness and gourmet quality.

## Comforts

Finally, after twenty-one months, I have shoes that fit and don't cause blisters. They were given to me by another inmate who realized they were too big for him, in exchange for two ziplock bags and a bowl of spaghetti. I had forgotten how good it feels not to have blisters. I'll add this luxury to my list of blessings.

Each day I marvel at the beauty of the brief but intense sunsets here. They are for me a personal sign of better and happier days to come.

---

> My Jesus, You suffice me for everything else in the world. Although the sufferings are severe, You sustain me. Although the times of loneliness are terrible, You make them sweet for me. Although the weakness is great, You change it into power for me. (*Diary*, 1655)

# 30

# October 1999

I am typing this newsletter on October 7, my fifty-seventh birthday. The "celebration" here at Club Fed was somewhat muted. No one knew or cared that I was reaching this wondrous milestone in my life. But all is well. My bland diet, hard work, daily naps, and twenty months of strenuous exercise have transformed my physical condition. The result is that I have gained more years in life expectancy than I have lost to confinement. So there, evil BOP!

## Crop Report

My little garden is still a source of surprises and pleasant distraction. I now have dozens of tomatoes on the plants, peppers by the handful each day, beautiful six-inch cantaloupes, thriving garlic, cucumbers harvested daily, and six-foot-tall citrus trees. Ingredients from the garden go into my Thursday night feasts.

Last week Chicken Cacciatore was the feature. It included a tub of pasta with garlic, oregano, Italian spice blend, and olive oil. It was delicious. There is usually enough for twenty to thirty hungry guys. It's not a pretty sight to watch, but every scrap disappears in no time at all. Dessert is bite-size Hershey bars and peanut butter cups from the commissary.

The dinners have also brought peace and quiet in the usually loud room next door. They have done more for race relations than any sensitivity session could. The tomato sauce is so thick and wonderful that I think I'll send Tony Angello the recipe. He can call it "Pollo in Pepper Sauce Penitentiary à la Carlo!"

The big problem with cooking in the dorm is maintaining a reasonable level of sanitation for cooking utensils and keeping food from spoiling. Five-gallon mop buckets filled with ice from the dorm's ice machine provide refrigeration, with the groceries kept in garbage bags under the ice. Washing dishes is usually done with laundry detergent in the bathroom sinks.

Special items like the foot tubs we cook in are given special care. My method of choice involves a safety office special combo of toilet bowl cleaner and SD-20, a strong detergent. This gives the cooking area a reassuring hospital smell and probably adds a little something to the sauce.

## Creative Burst

With all the recent dorm cooking, it became evident that small plastic spoons were not adequate. I decided to carve a large jambalaya spoon—and soon after, a large pasta fork—out of the cross beam in a freight pallet made out of beautiful old oak. I worked countless hours with chisels, Dremel tools, and mostly discarded sandpaper from the shop. My mother will be proud when she sees this work of art.

The spoon will be a good wedding gift for Beth. I hope she enjoys it and has occasion to reflect on its unusual genesis.

OCTOBER 1999

## Dental Denial

Once again I went in for BOP dental care (my sixth visit). Once again I got no care, no medication, and only vague suggestions of future treatment. I did have the benefit of a caring lecture, appropriate for a preschooler, chastising me for not having gotten earlier treatment.

I have written numerous requests for emergency care for my excruciatingly painful abscess. I get a visit scheduled but never any medication or treatment. Perhaps I will have some success before year's end. In the meantime, I have suffered serious bone loss that cannot be reversed. I will lose at least one tooth.

Thanks to all of you who have been so supportive and faithful. Please write when you can. Please also help the girls forget my absence from the weddings and celebrate enthusiastically our many blessings. Know that you are in my thoughts, prayers, and hopes for the future.

# 31

# November 1999

My absence from Beth and Rocky's wedding was a problem for the girls and for Joey, but it was not all negative. In fact, I had one of those strange and reassuring experiences during the wedding.

I spent the day reading, relaxing, and imagining what was going on at the wedding. During the actual time of the wedding, I was reading Gary Zukav's new book, *The Seat of the Soul*. Zukav postulates that relationships are often not what they appear to be. In his example, a father and daughter are separated physically for her wedding but are spiritually connected through their relationship and genuine love for each other. He proposes that the physically absent father can be more present than a physically present but aloof father.

Bingo! This explains the strange "connected" feeling that I have developed since being separated from everything and everyone I have cherished in the past. Through focused thought, letters, visits, and prayers sent and received, I am in fact more connected than I was when I was physically present and in the midst of everything.

## November 1999

An unexpected side effect of losing so much is the ability to focus on what I really have to be grateful for. This thought was a great consolation to me. It diminished my sense of sadness at being here instead of at home, where I belong.

To ice the cake, Beth and Rocky came to visit me on the Friday after the wedding. I eagerly took Beth out to the visiting yard to see the flowerbed planted by my roommate. The flowers spelled out, "Beth & Rocky, Dad Loves You," with a big flower heart. Beth's reaction was to burst into tears.

### More on Dental Care

My efforts to get some kind of treatment or medication for my aching tooth reached new heights of absurdity during October. I went back four times. On one visit, I got the dental assistant to look at my tooth. She was horrified when she saw that it had split into two large pieces, exposing the nerve and causing excruciating pain whenever it was touched. None of this or my eleven-month wait was enough to stir the dentist into action.

Finally, on my twelfth visit, by documented count, it was decreed that the tooth had to come out. I decided to postpone my extraction after watching the dentist extract the tooth of another inmate. But the dentist would not give me more time to think about it. He attacked me, as he had the prior patient, with the largest needle I have ever seen. There was intense burning as the Novocain took effect, followed by blessed numbness.

The hole in my jaw feels like the Grand Canyon, but the sweet relief came almost immediately. I am now completely recovered and can chew normally. I have also recaptured my sense of smell, thanks be to God!

# 32

# December 1999

Merry Christmas and Happy New Year to all! Here's hoping the much-ballyhooed arrival of the twenty-first century will be a non-event. I look forward with such eager anticipation to getting out of here that it would be truly irritating if the world ended before that happy day.

For reasons that seem difficult to fathom, it has become harder instead of easier to be here. I have to admit that it has begun to wear on me, and at times I feel as if the oppressive loneliness will never end. A sense that I am disappearing into a black hole of irrelevance sometimes overcomes me. But then another day dawns, and life goes on with a new sense of hope and renewed energy.

My Washington super-lawyers have asked the US Supreme Court to review my case. The time frame is uncertain, but there should be some response in three to six months. There seems to be a tidal wave of new and favorable legal developments. Most of the federal circuit courts hold that what I was accused of violating (state license laws, by secretly owning an interest in a client's business, which I did not own) isn't a crime under federal law. The

Supreme Court has also adopted new requirements of "materiality" for federal prosecutions based on the violation of state laws.

My trial judge refused to tell the jury about the materiality standard or to let them know what the Louisiana laws of ownership are before deciding the ownership issue. It is truly a strange world when information is allowed to be withheld, deliberately destroying my life and career.

I hope the Supreme Court will agree, but my chances are hurt, I believe, by the timing of the new developments. They have arisen after my trial and appeal, so I might be denied the benefit of the new decisions. In the meantime, I try not to permit myself the self-indulgent sop of becoming bitter about the injustice of it all.

I recently realized that part of my coping mechanism is to put the entire legal proceeding and the appeals out of my mind. I don't read the legal briefs, court decisions, and so forth. I may have gone overboard in this. Joey recently pointed out to me that she was totally unaware of the effort with the Supreme Court.

## Immediate Release for Jack

Rumor has it that after eight years of incarceration, Jack was ordered immediately released because he was sentenced improperly. Jack is one of the two exercise gurus here and a very nice person. It appears the system failed him.

Jack's guilt was seriously in doubt. On top of that, he got sixteen to eighteen years because the government faked the weight of the allegedly smuggled drugs in setting his sentence. No drugs were ever identified or found; Jack's sentence was based solely on testimony given by a drug dealer in exchange for a lenient sentence.

I did what I could to help him with his case, and I will feel great if the rumors turn out to be true.

## The Garden and Other Fun

The tomato plants are amazing. They are literally covered with huge green tomatoes, so much so that the branches are breaking under the strain. I'm hopeful that I can get a good cover over them when the first freezes come, so that we can keep them bearing all winter.

The garlic and cilantro crops are beautiful, and spices and herbs are doing well. The persimmon tree is now bare, thanks to the raccoons. The much-talked-about plans to tear down the building where the garden is located have come to naught so far, but disaster lurks around the corner. So I'm enjoying the garden to the max while it lasts.

My best new diversion are the several hours each day that I get to spend in the woodshop. I am making Christmas presents for the girls, and my major project is a wedding gift for Trish and Todd. This is taking a while.

The first step is to make boards to use in the project from freight pallets collected by the recycling team. Some of the stuff is really beautiful after it is cleaned up and planed. I have some great Lauan from South America as well as mahogany, red and white oak, and black walnut.

Each year various church groups come in to perform Christmas programs for the inmates. My personal favorite is the St. Joseph's Catholic Church Rock 'n Roll Full Gospel Choir. Most of the members seem to be related, and all can really sing.

## December 1999

When they cranked it up, not only did they rock and roll, but the ground literally shook. Doors and windows rattled. Shoes came off. Arms waved in the air. And a great mass of humanity began to move as if it were a single rhythmic organism. It was rollicking good fun. There were struts, shouts, ad-libs, laughs, tears, smiles, and lots of repetition. Everyone loved it.

The piano player reminded me of the ladies who play at Pat O'Brien's in the French Quarter. She did everything by ear and pounded the poor piano as it had never been pounded before. We hated to see this group leave.

# 33

# January 2000

With the new millennium, I have begun my third year in prison. Spiritually and mentally, my reading, meditation, and crossword puzzles are having a positive effect. I sometimes go for days without crying in public.

I've learned a great lesson in life: faith is essential and grows exponentially during times of extreme adversity. Each day brings things to dread—strenuous workouts, medical visits, counts, harassment by hacks—as well as things I eagerly anticipate, such as a good book, the Superbowl, visits, mail call, cooking, gardening, and woodworking. If time drags, I consider it a reprieve from the dreaded activity; and if time flies, it brings me closer to an anticipated event. So I am always content with whatever is, which is not a bad way to live.

Three days of freezing weather over the Christmas weekend killed all my tomato and pepper plants, but the harvest was plentiful. I kept 154 beautiful tomatoes and spread them all over the compound to ripen in various conditions of light and dark and

## January 2000

heat and cool. I use about six to eight tomatoes per week for my now-famous sauces, so I should have enough until spring.

As a result of my spreading culinary reputation, I was finally asked to assist in cooking a special New Year's Eve dinner. Two other lawyers were on the team. We were selected because the inmates hate all lawyers and justice system professionals, and this was our chance to atone for the sins of the entire profession.

The dish was to be Chinese fried rice with chicken and bamboo shoots. Cooking started on Thursday with hours of chopping, dicing, and slicing. We chopped a hundred pounds of turkey drumsticks and two bushels of onions, shredded mountains of carrots, ripped up fifty-five gallons of cabbage, diced a big box of green onions, and nipped the buds from two bushels of broccoli. The broccoli stems were peeled and sliced into faux bamboo shoots. We cooked a hundred pounds of raw rice.

On New Year's Eve, we started cooking at about noon. First we scrambled six hundred eggs; then we cooked all the vegetables; then we combined these and add rice and turkey. The final touch was a secret ingredient made of MSG, salt, and sugar with some soy sauce. This concoction was fried on the grill in forty-pound batches.

The inmates loved it, and I think I will be invited to be guest chef on a monthly basis. In February it will be chicken and sausage jambalaya and gumbo, I hope. In addition to the fun of learning to use the kitchen equipment, the quality of my dorm snacks has gone up considerably.

# 34

# February 2000

Sadly and unexpectedly, our warden died last Saturday. I had the unusual assignment of writing a eulogy for Mr. Myron Washington, which my boss will read at the memorial service.

The warden had known for a year that he was terminal, but he kept that from everyone. It was only about four weeks before his death that he became obviously sick. His is the sixth death among the staff since I arrived.

The warden never tolerated or engaged in harassment of inmates. Perhaps as a result of losing his protection, all dorms have been ripped apart this week in search of contraband. Much of what was seized and thrown away was of no consequence but might have violated some extension of an obscure rule (such as the ban on magazines over thirty days out of date). Sheets and blankets were torn apart. Extra socks and underwear over the official issue of three per inmate were discarded.

All manner of personal possessions were also seized. Extra sheets, blankets, and pillows were targeted. Coat hooks on lockers were removed. Shelves on the sides of lockers next to bunks were ripped out. All food was removed. Lights were confiscated.

FEBRUARY 2000

The problem is that there is no uniformity or predictability on what the hacks will confiscate, as each one interprets the rules as he chooses, without any control or review. It has made life more miserable than normal for many.

I was lucky. My bunk and locker were apparently handled by one of the hacks who likes me, as nothing was taken. This is a fringe benefit of being a veteran inmate. Some books that were controversial in the past were spared. The photo gallery on the side of my locker was untouched. No extra blankets or pillows were seized. My cooking stuff—which includes two large foot tubs, large pasta forks, jambalaya spoons, and a chopping board—was left behind.

Few were so fortunate. The misery created and the ill will needlessly generated are enormous. There is really no point to this. No weapons, drugs, or alcohol were seized.

## The New Bunkie

He is a white-bearded, scraggly-haired, jailhouse-tattooed, methamphetamine-manufacturing Florida native named "Gator" (something about killing an eight-foot gator barehanded while under the influence). So far he is quiet and considerate, at least by prison standards; and he has no obviously disgusting personal habits. Once his fanciful, tough-guy, prison veteran stories have been exhausted, peace will descend in the valley.

On my own case, a response is due February 10 from the US Solicitor General. Perhaps more delays have been requested. If not, some action could be forthcoming in the next thirty to ninety days.

But nothing is certain. I have learned to wait in units based on seasons rather than minutes, hours, or days. Maybe my time here has not been totally wasted after all.

## 35

## MARCH 2000

I have, at last, a new nickname to take the place of Dilbert, Erkel, and Achievement Man. It's "Mr. Green Jeans," due to my work with the plants. I have agreed to study the greenhouse operation during the two-month orientation period, after originally turning it down. If I do get the job, I am going to request a typewriter and desk in the greenhouse, so I can type while I commune with my photosynthetic friends. I know that my horticulturist mother and wife are pleased.

To my amazement, I have found that the job is a serious one. The mission is to grow 200,000 potted bedding plants per year, plus flowers and shrubs. Since the greenhouse holds "only" 10,000 plants in four-inch pots, plus about 20,000 sprouting seeds, it has to be turned over at least twenty times per year. The setup is a fully professional operation with sophisticated automatic watering, both inside and out.

The greenhouse manager is supposed to have two full-time assistants and a crew of about six for maintaining the flower beds.

## MARCH 2000

Most of these guys are invisible. But if I get the job full-time, I will probably be given a couple helpers whom I select.

In two weeks, I have already transplanted thousands of sprouts to individual pots with very low mortality rates. Our greenhouse eliminates the purchase of about $200,000 worth of flowering plants each year. Our expenses are less than $5,000, not counting the slave labor. Right now we are growing dozens of colorful annuals, bulbs, roses, vegetables, and palm and citrus trees. At least in theory, I can handle all these.

My advantage over most of the Navy personnel involved in landscaping is my willingness and ability to read about the plants we are growing. Most will survive no matter what we do to them.

My first day on the job, I dug up and made seven beautiful rows for a sprinkled vegetable garden. This year the dorm food will definitely improve. My peanut, rosemary, basil, and pepper crops are already in, and more peppers and tomatoes are sprouting. We will add cucumbers, cantaloupes, and even papayas soon.

Maybe you can already tell that I am excited about the greenhouse. It comes as close as possible to having some meaning to my life here. Every day there is something to look forward to. As I type this letter, I have 18,000 seeds sprouting; 10,000 flowers in pots in the greenhouse; 2,000 more pots in the shade house; 2,500 pots on outside shaded tables; and 4,500 pots in full sun on outside tables. All are automatically sprinkled three times a day in eight different zones. Soon I will be able to operate the timer, which looks to me like the instrument panel of an F-16.

## Back at the Zoo

With storage space at a premium in the dorm, I have designed and made a number of shelves for my locker—six in all! This adds greatly to my usable space and makes finding stuff easier. The shelves have become a big hit. I have made shelves of all sizes for other inmates and have gotten a kick out of the project.

Some guys think that the shelves are too nice and will be seized as contraband. I hope not. And so far so good, through at least six locker shakedowns.

My new bunkie has turned out to be bit of a strain. He pops lithium like jellybeans, talks wildly in his sleep, and feels a primal need to talk and tease continuously. He was scheduled to leave for the fabled drug program, but someone convinced him to turn it down and stay at Club Fed.

I'm not an expert, but his behavior is becoming stranger each day. His favorite new mannerism is to hold his finger to his lips and say "Shhh" to me a couple hundred times each day. So far I have not had any conversations with him that I have understood, so I pretend to be asleep and to read a lot. Avoiding eye contact seems to help.

Time is flying by. Mardi Gras is over, and Trish's wedding will be here soon. Easter is upon us.

Still no word about any aspect of my case. Hope springs eternal. I continue to hang on and hang in with some semblance of sanity remaining. At least I now have thousands of plants to focus on each day. Must go; time to water!

# 36

# April 2000

This has been quite a month for tumultuous upheaval and spectacular updates. After five years of consistently bad news, the prayers of many appear to have been answered in an unexpected way.

On the first day of spring, I was called by my supervisor and instructed without explanation to report to one of the secretaries. This almost always means some form of bad news, so I was a little apprehensive. I went to the office and found the person I needed. She said, "I have a message for you from your attorney, and I don't know whether this is good news or bad news."

She delivered a garbled message that made absolutely no sense. She had written down the message phonetically, and I finally deciphered the code: "The Supreme Court has *granted* a writ of certiorari in Mr. Cleveland's case," which means that they are going to hear my appeal!

Once I read the word "granted," I hyperventilated and then ran five miles on the track to avoid having a heart attack. I couldn't confirm the message until about eight hours later. While I wanted to believe that it was miraculously good news, I was afraid to even hope.

The court's decision to hear my appeal is momentous. The Supreme Court usually receives about ten thousand petitions a year, and they take seventy-five or so for a hearing. Among that blessed fraction, the court generally reverses about two-thirds. So my odds of a reversal have now changed from a hopeless long shot to an odds-on favorite!

My cause is boosted by the fact that of the eleven federal circuit courts of appeal, six have already held that what I have been given a ten-year sentence for is not a crime at all. This is unrelated to the fact that I didn't do what they claimed. Sadly, this latter fact is of little importance to the court, but my attorneys have assured me that my brief will emphasize my innocence anyway.

Only one circuit has held that what I am charged with is a crime (other than the Fifth Circuit, which is where my original appeal was heard). Three circuits have not considered the issue. In addition, I am told that the case in the Fifth Circuit has been severely criticized. Even more significant is the fact that my case will appeal to the conservative justices on the court, which is not true in most criminal cases.

Chief Justice Rehnquist has been calling on Congress to exercise restraint in enacting new criminal laws. In his view, criminal law is primarily an area of local or state concern. The Constitution created few federal crimes. But since the turn of the century, Congress has added about ten thousand new ones. This is excessive, and it bogs down the federal courts with cases that could more properly be prosecuted under state law.

Incidentally, state regulators do not consider my actions to have violated state law in any way and so testified at my trial. And Justice Rehnquist believes that federal laws need to be construed narrowly and not expanded beyond the clear initial intent of Congress. So the long and the short of it is that the news is gloriously and spectacularly good!

My attorneys assert that if I win in the Supreme Court, all charges against me will be dismissed, because they are at least indirectly based on alleged violations of state law. The government disagrees with the mysterious "tax conspiracy" count. Every tax return challenged by the prosecutors has been accepted by the IRS, and all my returns through 1998 have been formally audited or less formally reviewed without any changes.

The news gets potentially even better. My attorneys have filed a motion for my immediate release while I wait for the hearing, based upon the proposition that incarceration is not appropriate if there is a serious issue of law on appeal. Legal issues don't get any more serious than having the case selected for review by the US Supreme Court. A hearing will be held on April 27, 2000, to determine whether I will be granted bail pending appeal.

My biggest practical hurdle is that the judge who presided at my trial has a long, unbroken record of granting every government motion and denying every defense motion. So my optimism is realistically guarded. In the meantime, I continue in my struggle to maintain sanity and faith in a sea of uncertainty and turmoil.

## Garden Update

Since the Ides of March, I have been working full-time in the greenhouse, seven days a week. Most of my time is spent sprouting seeds and transplanting seedlings by the thousands. I have a great vegetable garden, potted plants, hanging baskets, and time for experimenting. It is truly soul satisfying and provides something to look forward to each day, with fantastic daily springtime growth.

My own little Garden of Eden is behind the greenhouse. It has a rose garden in spectacular full bloom; an aloe garden with lots of different varieties; a spice garden; ten rows of a vegetable garden; tables of annuals, perennials, wildflowers; and much more. There is an old broken park bench propped up in the middle of the garden near a birdbath made from a five-gallon drum. Doves, purple martins, hummingbirds, grackles, and squirrels seem completely tame and fearless. The squirrels wreak havoc, but we have so much that they never get it all.

The spot is very peaceful. I get up before daylight to water needy plants, then sit in the garden with a cup of coffee and enjoy the sunrise. These moments will be greatly missed if I am released, but I will try to find some way to cope. For now I spend hours trying to learn and get better organized. I may kill lots of plants, but I will at least do it systematically!

## Wedding Bells

The real headline this month was the wedding of Trish, daughter number four, to Todd at St. Joseph's Church. Although my attorneys made a valiant effort to have the judge consider my release on bail before the wedding, it was to no avail.

I terribly missed being at the wedding. However, the visiting yard here has been prepared with a special marigold patch that spells out "Trish (heart shape) Todd." I personally sprouted and transplanted the seeds, and I can't wait for the newlyweds to visit.

I am encouraged by recent events, and I continue to live in a cocoon of relative peace in a hellish environment. One of my coworkers has been having vivid prophetic dreams, even before I received the news from the Supreme Court, about my being released soon.

## April 2000

And my gardening job has brought me renewed hope. I can't resist passing on to you a quote from Marina Schinz, a noted photographer:

> To create a garden is to search for a better world. In our effort to improve on nature, we are guided by a vision of paradise. Whether the result is a horticultural masterpiece or only a modest vegetable patch, it is based on the expectation of a glorious future. This hope for the future is at the heart of all gardening.[1]

---

1  Jo Brielyn, *A Garden of Inspiration: Quotations for Lovers of Gardening and Growing* (Hobart, New York: Hatherleigh Press, 2015).

# 37

# KITTY: THE GREAT JUBILEE

"Thank you, Jesus! THANK YOU, JESUS!" After two years and four months of unjust imprisonment, my father was a free man.

The hearing with the trial judge to ask for his release while we waited for the hearing with the US Supreme Court was scheduled for the Thursday after Easter Sunday. Three days later we would celebrate the first official Divine Mercy Sunday, and Blessed Faustina would be canonized a saint! I couldn't believe the timing.

This was also the Great Jubilee year of 2000. In the Jewish and Catholic traditions, jubilee has meant the forgiveness of debts and *the release of prisoners*. When I learned that the hearing would start at three o'clock, the Hour of Mercy, it all seemed too good to be true. I was determined at that point to pray the powerful Divine Mercy Novena—nine days of prayer—with the special intention that my dad would be released from prison in time to celebrate Mass with our family on Divine Mercy Sunday.

When the day of the hearing finally arrived (the seventh day of my novena), I stayed busy at work and tried not to think about it.

But my stomach was in knots. At 3:30 p.m., my phone rang. It was my sister Beth, and she was sobbing.

"What happened?" I asked, my heart racing.

"Dad..." she cried. There was a long pause as she was overcome with emotion.

"Beth, tell me what happened!" I shouted into the phone, not really wanting to know now.

"Dad... is coming home!"

I wailed as the news sank in, my voice carrying down the hallway at work.

To our amazement, the trial judge had completely agreed with our position, and she ordered that Dad be released immediately. But since it would take hours for him to be processed out, and the prison office was closing in thirty minutes, we would not be able to get him until the next day.

Our plan was to meet in Slidell, Louisiana, and take one van to Pensacola, which was three hours from Slidell. We would stay at a hotel just minutes from the prison so that we could pick Dad up as soon as we were called. A few hours later, we congregated in the McDonald's parking lot in Slidell, where we exchanged long hugs, laughter, and many tears. Then my phone rang. It was Mel.

"Hey, is everything okay?" I asked.

"Yes, but hurry up," he said. "Your grandmother just called, and she said your dad is waiting at the gate!" It turned out that two benevolent women had done everything they could to process Dad out before the office closed at 4:00 p.m. So there he stood, just outside the prison gate, for almost six hours.

When we finally arrived, well after dark, Dad looked like a lost and forlorn orphan, clutching a brown paper bag with all his belongings. We jumped out of the van, smothered him in bear hugs and kisses, and pushed him into the van before anyone could say that they'd made a mistake.

We got home around 1:30 a.m. and were too excited to go to bed. Dad took us through stretching exercises, showing us how he could touch his toes with his palms flat after so many years of inflexibility. God makes all things new!

After a few hours of sleep, my father and Beth dropped in on some unsuspecting friends, then headed to the grocery store to prepare for his big feast. Dad marveled at the selection of fresh produce and the abundance of food, smiling at everyone he encountered. Beth said he looked like a lunatic, especially since he had to hold his pants at the waist to keep them from falling off his new slim physique. It was time to shop for new clothes, too!

Two days later was Divine Mercy Sunday. Our family celebrated Mass at St. Joseph's Church in New Orleans, where I was singing for the special celebrations for St. Faustina's canonization. I sobbed through the whole Mass. Later I shared our resurrection story with my fellow choir members as well as I could.

## Time for Some Fun

The week after my father's miraculous homecoming, his little fishing boat was ready to roll. Beth and I enthusiastically volunteered to be his first mates. He woke us well before dawn. Sandwiches and drinks were already packed in the big cooler, the boat and trailer hooked up to the truck, and the motor running. Sam, Dad's devoted black Lab, was glued to his side

We stopped at my father's favorite bait shop on Highway 23 to get frozen shrimp and fresh cockahoes (small fish that trout devour), then headed to Cypress Cove Marina. This was our launching point for the wide-open Gulf of Mexico.

"Hot *diggity!*" Dad exclaimed. "Look at all those boats. We're going to bring home some fish today!" By the time we got to Venice, several large commercial fishing boats were already heading out with their crew, a sign that the conditions were right for a good catch. "Kitty, I need you to back up the trailer while I get the boat in the water. Beth, I need you to take the rope and tie us up to the dock," he commanded.

Once we climbed aboard, Dad took us through the lush Mississippi River Delta and out into the Gulf. The sun was rising before us in magnificent shades of gold and pink, bathing everything in glory. I turned around to look at my father. His baseball cap was turned backward as we headed into the wind, and his expression was one of pure joy and wonder.

The hearing with the US Supreme Court, which was still six months away, might send him back to prison. But for now, Dad was reveling in the sweet taste of freedom, thanking God over and over again for answered prayers.

# 38

# MAY 2000: CARL'S LAST LETTER

This is the last installment, which I am writing from my Home Sweet Home. On Thursday, the 27th of April, the trial judge held a hearing on my motion for bail pending appeal with the US Supreme Court. At 3:30 p.m. that very day, the judge ordered me released from prison. By 4 p.m. I was free!

I left with nothing but the clothes I was wearing at the time and a small bag with a few books and letters. After a three-and-a-half-hour wait outside the prison gate, I began to get nervous. I was finally able to get in touch with my mother, who got word to Joey and the girls that I was waiting for them.

At 10 p.m. they arrived. I was in shock, and I remember little except a stop at Burger King for a snack and a late arrival at home. I do recall having us all do stretching exercises in the living room at 1:30 a.m. I was just a little ecstatic!

I have been trying to depressurize. I had never let myself even hope about being released, so it has taken time to adjust to being a civilian again. I have shopped recreationally for groceries, gone fishing several times, cleaned out the garage, sipped scotch on the rocks at sunset, attended dozens of AAU Biddy basketball games, played with Caitlin and the girls, visited friends, cooked and eaten good food, shopped for new clothes, worked on my boat, repaired Caitlin's go-kart, danced, prayed, cried, attended Kitty's hour-long live show on EWTN in Birmingham, gotten a physical, planted flowers, gone water skiing, gone to Mass frequently, visited lawyer friends and clients, gone on a short trip with Joey, and even found a little time for prison exercise routines.

Now I have to try to make sense of the whole experience and to decide what I am supposed to do with whatever is left of my life, at least until the Supreme Court decides my fate. For now I cannot practice law. So I shop, cook, wash dishes, do laundry, drive carpool, and go to Caitlin's practices. I'm having a ball! I don't see how I ever had time to work before.

As soon as the turmoil dies down, we will have a large gathering here at home to properly celebrate the miracle that you all share in as a result of your prayers, loyalty, and undying support. It will be a great "joint release" party, as we thank God for the release of Kitty's beautiful CD as well as my release from prison.

The title song of Kitty's CD, is "Surrender." I can't listen to it without crying—the painful memories are still so fresh. But the song is beautiful, inspirational, and insightful.

Hope to see everyone soon. Call, write, visit, or come stay for a few days. So far my life plan doesn't extend beyond the refreshing beverage I will have as soon as I finish typing.

# 39

## Paradise

In an exceedingly rare judgment, the US Supreme Court unanimously reversed my father's convictions, holding that what he had been accused of wasn't even a crime! Dad was home for good, the government could no longer demand that he pay money he didn't owe, and we could all begin the process of healing.

It would take a long time for Dad to be reinstated to the Bar Association and to the diaconate, so he did the next best thing: he went fishing, specifically as a fishing captain down in Venice. In short order, he earned his captain's license, found a beautiful boat with a fly bridge he named the Delta Dawn, and took charters out into the Gulf of Mexico and to his favorite fishing spot at the mouth of the Mississippi River. He was having the time of his life.

It was a special consolation to my dad when he was invited to the National Shrine of Divine Mercy in Stockbridge, Massachusetts, to share his miracle story. It was on Divine Mercy Sunday, with an estimated audience of 25,000 people. What a grace!

Back at home, Dad purchased a retired Acadian ambulance for Caitlin to drive to school. The entire basketball team fit in there, plus a barbeque pit for tailgating. And when my sister Beth gave him his very first grandson on October 7, his sixtieth birthday, it was almost more joy than he could take—especially after six daughters and five granddaughters!

But again, changes were coming.

# 40

# RESTORATION

Three years after his release, and just months after his sixtieth birthday, we received the news that my dad had a very aggressive form of prostate cancer—the same kind that had taken his father's life. He was told to get his affairs in order because he had only a few months to live.

We were all in shock. Prayer chains started in earnest. The doctors soon reported that—to their amazement—the cancer had not spread. Three years later, Dad was still with us.

In 2005, just a month before Hurricane Katrina, Mel and I joyfully welcomed a little girl into our family. We adopted Cecilia from China when she was sixteen months old. Since Dad had not yet been reinstated as a deacon, it was a true gift when the archbishop granted him special permission to baptize her.

Dad told us that he felt his last mission was to show us how to battle cancer bravely and, if necessary, to die with courage, hope, and grace. He did that and more.

Hurricane Katrina decimated his fishing enterprise under thirty feet of water and the family was exiled for months to Baton

Rouge, where Dad could continue to receive chemotherapy. But the cancer continued to spread, and it eventually metastasized to his bones and brain.

On Divine Mercy Sunday 2006, as I sang once again for the great celebration at St. Joseph Church in New Orleans, my dad accompanied me from a wheelchair. Sr. Briege McKenna, the nun with the gift of healing who had prayed over me years earlier, just happened to be in town and attending that Mass. She prayed with Dad for a miracle, and he was absolutely glowing afterward.

God's plans were different from ours, however. My father's body continued to decline rapidly. After three years of aggressive cancer treatments, it was time for us to tell him goodbye.

On a Saturday in July 2006, we girls came home to gather at his bedside. He had just been released from the hospital into hospice care, and we knew there wasn't much time left. A grief counselor came and shared some words of comfort.

"I just came from the vigil Mass," she began, "and the Scripture reading really made me think of your father. It's when St. Paul begs God to remove the thorn in the flesh, and God replies, 'My grace is sufficient for you. For power is made perfect in weakness.'"

We were astonished as the Holy Spirit pointed us once more to 2 Corinthians 12. God was assuring us that when all else has been stripped away, his grace is still enough—for my dad and for each one of us as well.

My sister Trish, a nurse by training, worked with the hospice nurse to make my father as comfortable as possible in the living room. We prayed the Divine Mercy Chaplet at his bedside, and a priest friend gave him last rites and the apostolic pardon. As we sang to him and rubbed his hands and feet with lotion, many friends and family came to pay their respects.

We all expected Dad to die that night, but the next day he was still with us. Since it was a Sunday, our priest friend celebrated Mass for us there at home. Dad was in and out of consciousness, but at the Sign of Peace he surprised us by sitting up in bed and speaking.

"I want to thank you all for coming here," he began, "and I apologize for my state of undress. But I want to encourage you to stick it out in your marriages. I love you all very much, and now I'm ready to die. So let's get on with it."

A couple days later, Dad was still holding on. As I sang the Divine Mercy Chaplet at his bedside, he slowly opened his eyes and looked at me.

"Kitty, why am I still here?" he whispered.

I gently patted his hand.

"I don't know, Dad. You keep rallying. You don't need to worry about Mom and Caitlin. I promise we'll take good care of them. You can go to Jesus, Dad. We'll all see you on the other side."

At that point he looked above my head, a bit to the left, and whispered, "Mom?" Then his eyes moved slowly to the right. "Dad?" He was between two worlds now. As another dose of morphine kicked in to manage his pain, he closed his eyes and fell asleep.

That same day, my sister Caroline, who was very pregnant with her first child, went into labor prematurely and had to be rushed to the hospital for delivery. My mother then made the difficult decision to tell her husband goodbye, for possibly the last time, as she headed to the hospital to be there for the birth.

Later at the hospital, as Mom accompanied Caroline during the hard labor, her cell phone rang. It was my dad's dear friend Dom.

"Joey, I have some wonderful news," he began, surprising her. "The Bar Association has just formally reinstated Carl as a lawyer.

And more importantly," he continued, "the archbishop has just reinstated Carl as a deacon."

My mother cried out with elation—her heart about to burst from the intense emotions of grief and joy, death and new life held so closely together. When we told my father the merciful update, his eyes opened wide. "Wow! God is so good," he whispered. And when Caroline got home from the hospital, she placed newborn Julia over his heart as he gently slipped into a coma.

About a week later, I rested my cheek on top of Dad's head for a long while, knowing from his breathing that it would be my last goodbye. These nine days of vigil at his bedside had permitted us to pray another Divine Mercy Novena for him. I knew that our merciful King was going to take him home.

I was gently awakened early the next morning by my mom. "Honey, your dad just died."

I went downstairs with the rest of the family, embraced my dad, and then went straight to his closet. I found his diaconate vestments in the back corner, carried them to the living room, and solemnly laid them out over his body. Dad was dressed in those vestments for the wake and funeral a few days later at St. Elizabeth Ann Seton Catholic Church, the place where he had served as a deacon for many years.

Over a thousand people came to pay their respects, and the Mass was standing room only. People were there not so much because of his successes but because of the witness he had given to hope in the Lord when all seemed lost. Many told us that his letters had inspired them and helped them keep the faith in their own struggles.

Dozens of priests and deacons also came to honor Dad's memory and pray for his soul. Denise Dupont, my father's brilliant young friend with cerebral palsy, delivered the eulogy. She eloquently demonstrated through her tortured body and inspired words what true strength and fierce loyalty look like.

A full choir came together to support my mother, who had long served as the choir director. And after Communion, my mom, five sisters, and I sang "Press On" by Bob Filoramo, harmonizing as only family can.

> For the man who follows Jesus all the days of his life,
> Who picks up his cross and walks with his God,
> A glorious inheritance awaits him at the end,
> When he will see and know his true Father,
> And the pearl of great price is in his hand.
>
> So as for me, I will press on in running the race,
> With my eyes fixed on Jesus, who inspires and perfects my faith.
> I will fight the good fight, with all my heart and soul,
> Till the day that I'm with Jesus,
> The day I'm finally home,
> The day that I have won the crown.

Thank you, Dad, for your brave example. I pray that I can make you proud and remember well the lessons you paid such a high price to teach me. May God reward you richly with the crown of life, till we meet again on the other side of the veil. I love and miss you.

*Kitty*

## Restoration

Eternal God, in Whom mercy is endless and the treasury of compassion inexhaustible, look kindly upon us and increase Your mercy in us, that in difficult moments we might not despair nor become despondent but with great confidence submit ourselves to Your holy will, which is Love and Mercy itself. (*Diary*, 950)

# 41

# An Invitation

The Lord Jesus made you for himself, he understands you perfectly, and his arms of merciful love are wide open to you. As St. Augustine writes in his *Confessions,* "You have made us for yourself, O Lord, and our heart is restless until it rests in you."

If you have yet to encounter God's merciful love, or if you just need a reminder, I invite you to say this prayer out loud:

> Lord Jesus, I need you. I believe in you; help my unbelief. Please have mercy on me, Lord. Forgive me for the evil I have done and the good I have failed to do. Help me make amends for the suffering I have caused others, have caused myself, and have caused you. With your help, I choose to forgive those who have hurt me. Heal me, Lord, and give me the joy of your abiding presence, your faithful friendship, and your merciful love. I open my life to you. Amen.

Jesus, I trust in you!

# Postscript

I'm thrilled to report that my mom, Joey, married a wonderful man a few years after my father's death. Mike "Pops" Caruso is the exact opposite of my father in temperament, and I believe he was hand-picked by my dad to make her immensely happy with the remaining years of her life. We all know that she deserves it! We have also given them plenty of grandchildren to dote on—fifteen at the last count.

Connie currently lives in North Canton, Ohio, and has a flourishing Christian counseling practice that she does both online and in person (www.waymakercpc.com). You can also find her in the garden and reporting on the northern weather, which is so very different from Louisiana.

My sisters Beth and Caroline live just a few minutes from me on the north shore of Lake Pontchartrain, a short distance from our mom. Beth is a part-time real estate agent, is president of the Louisiana PTA, and is a team member of Rachel's Vineyard, a powerful healing ministry to men and women who have lost children through abortion or miscarriage (www.rachelsvineyard.org).

Caroline has a thriving Christian counseling practice that she does both online and in person (www.waymakernola.com). When not attending to her many responsibilities, you can also find her frolicking in the garden.

Trish and Caitlin both live in California. Trish is a talented seamstress and has a gorgeous shop of custom bed linens and clothing in Fullerton (Instagram: @cottagebydesign). In her free time, she is in her rose garden sipping coffee.

Caitlin recently founded Match, a nonprofit in Mendocino County to provide enrichment for autistic young adults, coaches AAU basketball, and regales us with hilarious stories of life in Fort Bragg, which contains perhaps even more characters than New Orleans.

As for me, I founded a nonprofit called Sounds of Peace to give all of my recorded music away to the poor, the sick, and the dying at no charge to them. You can read the miracle story behind it, read some amazing testimonies of healing, and listen to all of my music for free on my website. As of this writing, you can find me most weekday mornings leading a scriptural rosary at 5:45 a.m. CT on YouTube and Instagram with different spontaneous meditations every day. You are cordially invited to join our wonderful growing community of Morning Glories! It would be our delight to pray with you and for you.

*End*

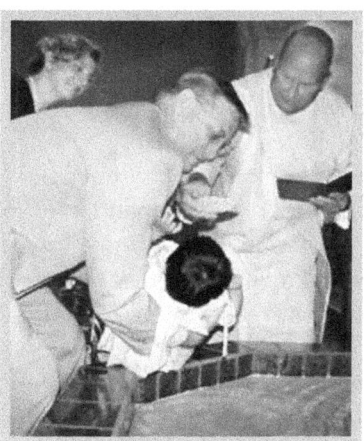

# Acknowledgments

This book would not have been possible without the love and support of my husband, Mel, my daughter, Cecilia, my mom, Joey, my stepdad, Mike, and my sisters Connie, Beth, Trish, Caroline, and Caitlin. I also owe a debt of gratitude to Immaculée Ilibagiza for motivating me to finish this labor of love by offering to write the foreword; to Angelle Albright for transcribing my testimony so many years ago and for her encouragement to keep going; to Mary O'Neill for her expert editing and kindness; to Claire Dwyer for her guidance in memoir writing and for her encouragement-through-tears after reading it; and to Sr. Briege McKenna for being such a light in my life.

Big thanks also to Kelly Wahlquist for introducing me to Beth McNamara at *The Word Among Us Press*; to Dan Burke for reading the book and going to bat for me; to Jeff Cavins for giving me a shot so many years ago; to Johnnette Benkovic Williams for her years of friendship, love, and guidance; to all the friends who read and reviewed this book; and to Beth, Jessica, April, and James at *The Word Among Us Press*—you have been a delight! I must also thank the priests who have true friends and spiritual fathers to me over the years, especially Fr. Philip Scott, Fr. Robert Cavalier, Pope St. John Paul II, and the late Fr. Harold Cohen, who taught me about St. Faustina and the Divine Mercy of Jesus so many years ago.

Finally, I want to thank the Morning Glories who have been praying with me and for me the last four-plus years, as well as the thousands of people who have supported my dreams with their donations and prayers over the last twenty-five years. I truly could not have done it without you! May God richly reward you for your kindness and generosity.

# About the Author

Kitty Cleveland is a singer/songwriter, inspirational speaker, and artist from New Orleans who began her professional career as a lawyer and then as a college instructor. In an Adoration chapel one day in 1998, as she searched for God during a devastating family crisis, she clearly heard the Lord Jesus call her to become a "music missionary." Kitty ultimately released ten CDs of music and prayer, which became the foundation for her nonprofit, Sounds of Peace. This ministry is devoted to sharing the consolation of her music and prayer with those who are poor, sick, and dying, at no charge to them.

To learn more about Sounds of Peace and to stream Kitty's music for free, please visit **www.kittycleveland.com**.

## A Note from Kitty

If I had to boil down the essence of what I feel called to do, it is to *encourage* people—whether through singing, storytelling, painting, or teaching from the great Catholic spiritual writers and my own life experience. Tears and laughter from the audience (and from me) are not uncommon, and I consider them to be a true gift of the Holy Spirit. These audiences have ranged from Catholic women's conferences to leadership groups to large family conferences.

My heart burns with a desire to share the riches of our Catholic faith, especially to lapsed or lukewarm Catholics, and I love to do it in a sincere, creative, light-hearted way. I submit myself to the teaching authority of the Magisterium of the Roman Catholic Church in matters of faith and morals, and I delight in her guidance.

Favorite topics include:

1. His Grace Is Enough (2 Corinthians 12:9)
2. Beloved: Finding My Identity in Christ (for women)
3. Deus Providebit: Trusting in God's Divine Providence
4. The Habit of Prayer: Making Time for God
5. Mary as Mediatrix: Discovering Who the Virgin Mary Is for You *Personally*
6. Peace I Leave with You: How to Enjoy the Peace of Christ in an Anxious World
7. Divine Mercy: A Miracle Story

For bookings, please reach out through my website contact page at **www.kittycleveland.com**. And if this book blessed you, I'd love to hear about it! My email is **kitty@kittycleveland.com.**

**To stay in touch via social media:**
**Instagram**: @kittycleveland
**YouTube:** www.youtube.com/kittycleveland
**Locals:** kittycleveland.locals.com
**Facebook**: Kitty Cleveland Music

# Sounds of Peace

On August 28, 2019, I had one of those inspirations that would change the course of my life. I had just sung for my second funeral in three days, and both families told me that they had been playing my CDs for their loved ones as they took their last breaths. I'm always humbled by these stories, and as I was praying about how I might share my music with even more people, I heard a sweet voice say to my soul, **"Give your music away to the poor, the sick, and the dying. No one should suffer or die without consolation."** I was filled with joy as the details came quickly for downloading all nine of my Christian CDs onto portable MP3 music players and then distributing them by the thousands to those in need.

The month after the first 2,000 players arrived, Covid-19 hit the U.S. While many were "suffering and dying without consolation" during that time, we were able to distribute the players in bulk to hospitals and nursing homes. Then I received my first letter:

> *Dear Kitty,*
> *I was in the hospital with Covid-19 [struggling for my life], and the nurse brought me one of your Sounds of Peace players. Little did I know that my life would change right then and there. As soon as I turned on the music, I felt all the doubts, fears, and sickness leave my body. I was inspired, at peace, and felt loved by God. Then the doctor came in a little while later and said, "You look too healthy to be here. Would you like to go home?" I started crying again with joy and relief.*
> *Thank you so much for the gift of your music. —P.V.*

If you would like to read other testimonials and stream my music straight from my website (it's free!), please visit **www.kittycleveland.com**.

**The Word Among Us** publishes a monthly devotional magazine, books, Bible studies, and pamphlets that help Catholics grow in their faith.

To learn more about who we are and what we publish, visit www.wau.org. There you will find a variety of Catholic resources that will help you grow in your faith.

Your review makes a difference! If you enjoyed this book, please consider sharing your review on Amazon using the QR code below.

*Embrace His Word*
*Listen to God . . .*

**www.wau.org**

www.ingramcontent.com/pod-product-compliance
Lightning Source LLC
Chambersburg PA
CBHW070058080526
44586CB00013B/1111